A Matter of
Life or Death

Why Black Men Must Save
Black Boys in America's

Public Schools

Dr. Michael W. Nellums
Dr. Walter Milton, Jr.

Black Male Educators Share Their Stories

One-L Group

Published by

One-L Group

PO Box 21815

Nashville, TN 37221

United States of America

Cover photograph by John Fortunato.

Printed in the United States of America.

Contributions by:

Henry Kleckley

Mr. Jeremy Owoh ABD

Mr. Marquis Cooper Sr. ABD

Mr. Milo Austin

Dr. John Gilliame

Mr. Floyd Williams

Dr. Charles Hopson

Mr. Jackie Calhoun

Mr. Don Booth

Mr. Rex Deloney

Dr. Darnell Bell

Mr. Sydney Jordan

Dr. T.C. Wallace, Jr.

Mr. Larry Hemingway

Dr. Reginald Wilson

Mr. Duane Clayton

Mr. Saleem Osman Bilal

Sam McNabb

Acknowledgments - Dr. Michael W. Nellums

Almost ten years ago, my mother had a stroke. I remember watching her lay in a hospital bed connected to monitoring equipment, afraid I might lose her. She got worse before she got better and stayed in the hospital for more than a month. My mother never gave up; six weeks after her stroke, she left the hospital on her own terms – she was a little weak but determined to live life to the fullest.

I draw great strength from my mother who, despite all of her pain and suffering, continues to fight and live life. She has a quiet strength and dignity about her that I, along with others who have felt her kindness, appreciate greatly. My mother has always been, and continues to be, my greatest supporter. I consider myself fortunate and blessed to have her as my mother for the last fifty years.

There are many others who have encouraged and inspired me over the years. Abraham Woodard was the principal of the all-black school system in my hometown. He was not only well educated and independent, but he never uttered a word when I borrowed the newspaper out of his yard every morning, read it, and threw it back two hours later! He was a proud man who never let anyone see him sweat. Educated, sophisticated, well dressed and well spoken, Mr. Woodard was a Renaissance Man long before the term became popular. I now can fully appreciate having the skills to deal with those educated folks as well as the street fools, and never change clothes in the process.

Mrs. Thelma Sanders, Mrs. Alma Thornton and Mrs. Eunice Stennis were three of my favorite teachers. They nurtured this black, poor boy from living on the edge of the Delta to becoming a professional broadcaster and eventually Dr. Nellums. Between the three of them, I never heard one negative word about the possibilities for my life and all that I might accomplish. All young black boys deserve the loving, nurturing environments that these three educators created in their classrooms. I continue to admire the work they did and try to replicate their good works with my children daily.

Dr. Richardson, Ora and Dr. Taylor are people who stand up for who and what they believe in. I owe them a tremendous debt of gratitude. Ora, I appreciate your sage wisdom and advice. Dr. Richardson is a sister, mentor, and mother all rolled into one. Dr. Taylor taught me about my moral responsibility to give back to young black men. My introduction to my own history came from his hands, his wisdom, and his example of black fatherhood.

Don, Mr. O, D. Bell, Rex, Dr. G, Henry, Marquis, Reggie and Jackie, and the late Dr. Hopson took the time to share their stories with me about the positive influence that they as black men can have on these young lost brothers. Their support for this project was immeasurable.

My son Michael is the joy of my life. Son you inspire me and make dad so proud. Brenda thank you for loving and caring for our son Michael. You are a great mother and I appreciate all that you did to help keep our young black son on the right track during those formative years.

In closing, we all have one major inspiration that compels, encourages and disappoints, and I had one, too. Parker, thank you for believing in me and then leaving me to suffer alone in that terrible thunderstorm. As I watched the waters around me rise, and floated helplessly without a life jacket in that raging river, I looked up and saw you watching from the safety of the covered bridge. I will never forget that moment, and am eternally grateful to God for allowing me to live and tell this story. On that day, I learned that some friendships don't always last a lifetime.

Acknowledgments - Dr. Walter Milton, Jr.

I am thankful to Almighty God for giving Dr. Nellums and me the vision and the ability to create this important book. I appreciate all of the individuals who participated in the project as well.

I am grateful to have been blessed with a loving family who continues to exemplify unyielding patience, laughter, support and commitment as I work diligently to achieve my desired aspirations. My wife Lisa has given me undying love, dedication and friendship – our bond is everlasting. My children – Nathaniel Walter Milton, Omari Mekhi Milton, Ezana Haben Milton and Adrianne Jade Milton – love and believe in me, and I feel the same way about them.

My six sisters and my brother have helped me to become the man I am today.

My parents, Walter and Louise Milton, are no longer with us, but their spirits and love shower me every moment. They taught me the essence of what it is to be a good human being and poured excellence into my soul. Jewel Petros loves and cares for my family and I. She means a great deal to my crew and me.

My nieces and nephews continue to be a motivation to me, and I hope that I am modeling an image that is pleasing to them.

As I said before, I have been very fortunate to have had in my life, and still have, many wonderful cheerleaders and nurturers to help me navigate life's curves and, sometimes, roadblocks. There are too many to name, but they know who they are. Again, I say thank you for being able to give me exactly what I needed when I needed it.

Like always, I am reminded of the songwriter's words, "I don't feel any ways tired, because He has brought me too far to leave me!"

Thank you Father, Mother-God; your spirit, grace and mercy still carry me through. Peace, blessings and love to all of my ancestors who paved the way, smoothed my path and hydrated my soul. Thanks for bending and allowing your backs to be bridges so that I could cross the troubled waters.

I would like to give a special shout out to my business partner and the entire From the Heart International Educational Services family. Peace!

Contents

Prologue

When I think about the plight of black boys as they matriculate, mature and transcend to young adulthood and eventually to manhood, I think of my three biological sons and the millions of other boys who share my hue. I am bombarded by numerous thoughts about this battlefield that we have so elegantly entitled "The World." I say this because life for many black boys is akin to a war. Wars on their minds, souls, spirits and yes, even their bodies take place on a daily basis. It is my desire that our sons become equipped with an artillery of excellence, weapons of mass knowledge/information and a navigation/GPS system that will help them avoid life's roadblocks. In fact, it is my sincerest hope that they will travel down roads where the course of their lives will serve as testimonies that would cause our ancestors to rejoice and marvel.

Too many black men find themselves in a mad race against time. Unfortunately, right when we think we are progressing, we realize we are experiencing the "treadmill effect" – moving swiftly but simply not going anywhere because we are strapped by the psychological chains of slavery. We are contending with things we cannot articulate because we are fighting forces that were systemically placed to keep us neutralized. When one is acting out such a psychosis of psychological slavery, there is a high probability that internalized racism, self-destruction, self-degradation, intrinsic aggression and self-hate (black on black destruction) will linger, dwell and eventually find a home.

John Henrik Clarke, educator, historian, writer, scholar, lecturer, researcher and one of the greatest men who ever lived, once said, "We are a nation, within a nation, looking for a nationality." I often would say we are victims of forced amnesia. Dr. Clarke clearly stated, "More critically, why do so many of us have a God-Concept assigned to us by other people. No people can be whole without an understanding of their history and this history must begin with a definition of their history." Dr. Clarke concludes with the following:

To me history is the clock that people use to tell their political and cultural time of day. It is also a clock that they use to find themselves on the map of human geography. The role of history in the final analysis is to tell a people where they have been and what they have been, where they are and what they are. Most importantly, the role of history is to tell a people where they still must go and what they still must be. To me the relationship of a people to their history is the same as the relationship of a child to its mother.

Dr. Clarke got it right. I believe there is a direct correlation with one knowing self from a historical context and his/her ability to see this grandiose experience we call life through its proper lenses. This increases one's probability of living a peaceful life that is prosperous, purposeful and beneficial to the larger human family.

If our boys find out who they are and where they come

from, and the many Godly contributions their people made to civilization, then they will excel even more in every aspect of their lives. They are the decedents of the movers and shakers of the universe. Men of African descent did not arrive on the scene from a monolithic ancestry but an ancestry of variety, colorfulness, beauty, strength, brotherly love, self-consciousness, richness, perseverance, kingship, integrity, honesty, righteousness, respect for self and others, strength, wholeness, intelligence, brilliance, responsibility, and a commitment to family. We are recipients of a very painful, distinguished, diverse, and victorious culture and history. By nature, we are a collective people despite our uniqueness and differences.

As a former school superintendent and currently providing services as a consultant, I have been blessed with the opportunity to work with educators, parents and students throughout the country, and I often am amazed how schools are ill equipped to work with black male students. This often results in a major disconnectedness between black male students and many of the people who are responsible for educating them. I must say that in many cases it has nothing to do with an educator's lack of caring or intentions, but everything to do with ineffective approaches to educating these particular students.

I vividly remember talking to students in the Pulaski County Special School District about the quality of their education and the experiences they were having. One student made the following poignant statement, "In school we learn so much about other cultures, particularly whites, and if you are not careful, you would think they invented air." He continued by asking simple, yet profound questions, "What happened to us before we got on the boats against our will to come here? Who were we and how did we live and exist?"

The answers to questions such as these guide the essays collected in this book. The co-author of this book, Dr. Michael Nellums, an accomplished educator currently serving as a high school principal for Pine Bluff High School, and I are dedicated to creating a resource for parents, students and community members. Our work in urban environments or environments populated with black male students has propelled us to join in the pursuit to write this book. Through our long and intense conversations regarding black male students and the current state of affairs pertaining to public education and these students, we decided to have a meeting of the minds and co-author what we believe to be a necessary read for all people concerned about our boys.

Although we both are individuals who care about all students in general, we decided to particularly focus on black males. Combined, Dr. Nellums and I have well over 40 years of service in the field of education. Those years have been laborious and dedicated to making a positive and lasting impact in the lives of students. This book not only comprises testimonials from black males in education, but also solutions. It is our firm belief that readers will find our project meaningful and helpful in their fight to combat the numerous and varied challenges that impact our boys. Lastly, it is my hope and desire that we can provide a unique and thought-provoking perspective that will serve as the basis for a most sacred and necessary discussion about and amongst black men who are deeply concerned about and committed to the education of black boys.

Dr. Walter Milton, Jr.

Chapter One

Saving Our Sons

*Our generation must inform and teach young
black boys how to become productive black men
in the communities they call home.*

Michael W. Nellums, Ed.D

High School Principal
Public School Board Member

If not me, then who? If not us, then why? If not now, then when? This was my very personal response to a group of college-educated, professional African American men who had gathered to discuss the plight of things with black boys in public schools and private prisons across the great state of Arkansas.

We were attending a professional development conference and lamented the lack of progress we observed in the scores of African American boys in the yearly testing conducted by the Arkansas Department of Education. The spin was on –

trying to convince the public that black boys and girls were making some progress. It was ugly listening to and watching the presenter display an awkward level of discomfort as she gleefully exclaimed, "Black kids overall scored ten points higher than the year before." However, most still were below basic. Silently, I thought, "You have got to be kidding me!" Black boys move up ten percent from the bottom, and white kids at the top and in the middle move up twelve percent. I then had my Morgan Freeman moment, shook my head in disbelief and told the brothers at the table, "That means that most black kids can barely read."

The presenter continued: "Black boys improved roughly two percent in one area and three percent in another, and black girls gained five percent to top off the scoring." What was not said was that these scores still equated to an average performance rating of below basic.

This simply meant that the test-takers' academic skill level placed them in a category that was below a level most Americans consider basic for one's survival. This was my moment to pause and reflect, and so I did just that. I reflected on my faith and my never-changing belief that things would improve if we just keep believing and pushing.

In the last several years, I have had many occasions to lean on my faith. I do believe that God lives in all of our lives, but I also believe that the devil stays busy by creating negativity and pessimism to keep us off balance and hinder progress. Once in the midst of a personal storm, I had a faith-filled moment and found inspiration in the following words of Stephen Kraggwa – "Try and fail, but don't fail to try." This quote captured the essence of my life's journey; it also captured my quest to find my purpose. I reflected, "Could this be my call to action?" Yet, as quickly as this inner peace settled over me, fear seemed to appear in the rear view mirror, threatening to paralyze my progress. Self-doubt crept in and tainted my purpose.

"Where do I start? What resources do I have? Am I my own personal guide and GPS system to navigate this uncharted territory?" It was raining in my house. The area that housed my soul was wet. I was traveling in a heavy thunderstorm, yet my faith covered me. My faith became my guiding light, removing all clouds of uncertainty.

The solution for my self-doubt came quickly. Deep within, I concluded I must start by willingly taking the first step… alone. I could not become paralyzed by fear. The Chinese writer, Lyn Yutang, wrote, "Hope is like a road in the country; there was never a road, but when many people walk on it, the road comes into existence." His words mirrored my personal journey as an African American student, teacher and father. My advocacy for the uplift of young black males in public schools was simply an outgrowth of my own experiences as a young black boy. More than thirty years earlier, I experienced the gift of hope from another black man, Dr. Theman Taylor, Sr., who cared about young black people and this particular young black boy and his future. Less than eighteen months ago, I received a similar gift from another black man, the late Dr. Charles Hopson. Twelve months ago, it was Todd Speight, David Bowser, Jerry Payne, Herman Horace, Ken Dickson and Harold Jackson.

I am grateful daily for these people. According to psychologist Robert Emmons of the University of California, gratitude is defined in two parts. First, it is an affirmation of goodness in the world and second, gratitude requires the recognition that the sources of this goodness exists outside of individuals. I believe people often appear in our lives for purposes unknown at the time of their entry. I have experienced many of these people. Some were tremendous influences who made significant contributions and had a measurable impact on my life. Others were distractions, mere speed bumps, obstacles and thorns in my flesh that I was forced to overcome. We all have these distractions in our lives, but we cannot allow them to deter us from traveling the path of personal accomplishment and fulfillment.

While I pursued the highest level of education, a classmate convinced me that the measure of success in my life would be determined by my ability to reach beyond my personal comfort zone. My willingness to travel a different path might make a difference not only in my life but in the lives of others. As quietly as I met Hope, she vanished. There was no opportunity to say goodbye or to reflect on time spent together. She simply disappeared, and left me to reflect on the words of Ralph Ellison who stated, "When I discover who I am, I'll be free." My process of discovering my true cause, my true conviction and my purpose had begun.

"When I discover who I am, I will be free" echoed in my mind, turning over and over. However, one cannot plough a field simply by turning it over repeatedly in the mind. My resolve became that my actions did not always have to be the right choices or reflect good timing; I simply needed to plough the ground. I had to move, and move now. My steps had to be about action and not weighed down by inertia. A decision was made to match my thoughts and deeds to my commitment to help young black males excel in public schools across this country.

Fear is a dark shadow that envelops and ultimately imprisons us within ourselves. We've all been a prisoner at one time or another, dealing with the unknown, rejection, misunderstandings and uncertainty. Yet, we forget that while we are temporarily trapped in a storm, we are not stuck. I will reference the book of Matthew, Chapter 8, Verses 24-27, "When the storm rages in your life, how will you respond?"

In public schools, private prisons, and state-supported retraining, reformatory and rehabilitation institutions, the crisis at hand is real. Black boys are being treated with band-aid approaches, yet the hemorrhaging cannot be stopped with a band-aid. To obtain an accurate diagnosis and solution, the intricacies and complexities of a black boy's academic, societal and genetic makeup must be examined at the microscopic level. It is malpractice to camouflage the system's inability to comprehend the complexity of black boys' academic and social conditions. Yet, Black America tolerates, encourages and even sustains the systems that create this permanent underclass of black boys.

The unwillingness of public schools and other institutions to even acknowledge failure of this endangered species is alarming. There appears to be no genuine or sustained effort to develop authentic, innovative and viable solutions to assist black boys academically or socially. At the end of the day, this visible lack of readiness not only prevents black boys from being productive and contributing members of society, but it creates and sustains a viable threat to Black America's own posterity and our communities at large.

On average, black boys graduate from public schools in the United States reading at about an eighth grade level. While that represents an average reading level, many black boys read far below that level. For black boys, poor reading skills often translate into poor verbal skills. Black boys become foreigners in their own native land. They live in a society that places a premium on written and spoken language, yet they do not have, nor will they ever acquire, the ability to effectively communicate.

For young black boys, slang becomes the accepted vernacular. Speaking in rhyme or riddles is what I often call it; rapping their way through life. Everything has a beat for young black boys. The latest rap phrase or lyric becomes a substitute for meaningful conversation. I often think that when a young black boy has great difficulty communicating effectively, somewhere, some coward silently claps and cheers for the unfortunate demise of yet another young brother. We must demand better.

Below basic language skills inhibit black boys from reading and understanding basic information necessary to comprehend test questions, apply for college, apply for jobs, pay taxes and read contracts. As a matter of law, public education entities publish school district summary reports. Sadly, most have reached the same unfortunate conclusion. The achievement gap is not closing, and more black boys are falling farther behind. Whether urban or rural, the statistics are the same. Black boys are fairing poorly on any and all meaningful assessments in this country. While others have made an effort to examine the problem, the terrible reality by and large is that black men in America have abdicated the responsibility of preparing black boys for life.

As black men we have given away the one responsibility that our culture deems essential to the survival of our race – rearing black boys. Our generation must inform and teach young black boys how to become productive black men in the communities they call home. The media, including television, radio, sports and entertainment, must be disconnected, and black boys must tune into the reality of a world where only a black man can teach a black boy what it feels like to grow up, struggle and succeed as a black man.

Though I am far from perfect, I understand purpose. Forty-plus years of walking around this planet with coffee-colored skin, has produced passion and purpose. I have encouraged those who share their stories to speak their truth with that same passion and purpose. Over the last 40 years, black men have endured tremendous pain not only in American society but also in public institutions of learning, so-called schoolhouses. How we really feel and how our sons have lived with the weight of poor to no academic achievement rests squarely on our collective shoulders. These stories cannot be discounted. They must be included in the annals of history, for both society and public schools.

The charge is to call it like they see it now – to dissect the challenge, shine a light on the opportunity and become conductors on the underground railroad for black boys who otherwise would not reach their potential. Harriet Tubman said, "I have freed a lot of slaves, I would have freed even more if they knew they were slaves." This statement is true today for not only young black men, but for many African Americans who are in positions to make a significant difference in the lives of young brothers.

This text is not conversation for a social mixer and therefore let us not mince words with those who seek to quantify, qualify and otherwise intellectualize the average primary caregiver out of the conversation. The failure of black men to address the failure of black boys in public schools is criminal. For black men of all walks of life to appear at a child's conception and disappear for formative manhood training is Willie Lynch-style legalized genocide. As a slave master, Lynch sought to keep the slaves under control for generations by breaking their spirit. They were taught distrust and to pit Black against Black. A sense of inferiority and interdependence on the master became acceptable. Envy and distrust of thy brother overruled the ability to plan a solution or escape from the jaws of the oppressor.

Black boys have been caught in a vicious cycle of lip service. Everyone speaks only to be heard and not to be difference makers who bring real solutions to the table. Policies produced and practices implemented by people with no vested interest in solving the problem of low black male achievement have not only become prevalent but standard fare. Three hundred years later, the spirit of Lynch still haunts Black folk. We are as divided by skin tone, perceived economic status and dependency on others as our ancestors were three hundred years ago.

We let others kill our children's hopes and dreams without question and with a spirit of acceptance that indicates, "They know best." If you teach a black man that he can never walk through the front door because the side or rear doors are acceptable entry points, then he always will settle for the second best point of entry. He will always think that living in the projects was good enough for his mother and his grandmother, so it should be good enough for his son, too. He will continue to buy used items. He will not seek higher education or vocational training because he has been told that getting a job, not establishing a career, is what really matters.

For centuries, we as black men have robbed our black boys of their aspirations. We have agreed to this nonsense by silent acceptance and acclamation. If you accept the terms and conditions of slavery even while you are free, then you remain a slave.

In educational terms, we speak of root cause analysis. This technique helps people answer the basic question of why this problem happened in the first place. For young brothers lost in this vicious cycle, we first must identify the three W's before we apply the balm. We must determine the what, why, and how to do, to prevent a reoccurrence. Root cause analysis assumes that systems and events are interrelated, and that three major causes represent the foundation for most problems, including those occurring with black boys in public schools. For the purpose of this work, we will focus on human causes, where people did something wrong or did nothing at all, and organizational causes, where processes that people use in public schools are faulty, and no one bothers to do systematic checks to make sure that these processes are actually effective.

Though several problems relating to black boys have been identified in public schools and numerous data has been collected, the important third step in root cause analysis often is overlooked. If these institutions and those responsible for creating and implementing policy and processes would simply look to determine potential causes, they might easily identify the sequence of activities in the lives of black boys that created their current status. More importantly, schools might identify why these problems continue to occur and why cookie cutter solutions just will not work for black boys.

There are no trademark infringement concerns with telling it like it is, so we must ask the following questions. Why have black men largely become silent partners in the social and academic development of black boys? While many teachers know content, they teach through a lens that does not integrate the impact of culture. Why must we wait when absolute failure is imminent? The voice of black men must resound loud and clear and summon a call to action.

For black men, intervention with black boys sooner than later is no longer an option. Organized government entities have failed at every level to make inroads into eradicating the disease that is destroying black males at a higher rate than all crimes and sexually transmitted diseases combined. The perils of living as black men and boys, with the daily threat of mass unemployment and incarceration, demands intervention now, or we face the certainty of cultural insignificance or even worse, extinction.

In my life, I have been blessed with a season of change. If you are a spiritual person of any color, you will understand that statement. If not, then my prayer for you is that when you read this collection of essays written by men of color who choose to educate, you will experience your season and be moved to action. Perhaps you are a black brother, father, neighbor, doctor, lawyer, bricklayer, etc. Regardless of occupation, your collective experiences equal the sum total of who black men are and the faces they represent in this society. Your willingness to share and prepare young black boys in public schools is crucial. If you are a black woman with a teenage daughter, you have everything riding on this season of change for black boys.

It is time to move beyond the place others have declared to be, our final resting place. While college-educated professionals are not the norm in most black communities, those of us who are have the greatest obligation to move our people forward. However, dealing realistically with the crisis at hand requires an extraordinary leap of faith. Arthur Ashe stated, "True heroism is remarkable, sober, and very un-dramatic. It is not the urge to surpass all others at all costs, but the urge to serve others at all costs." I count my blessings daily, and I am grateful and remain optimistic about my people. While form is important, the soul of black folks is what really matters.

I hope you join me in this journey to save our black boys.

Chapter Two

Exercise your Gift

It is going to take courage, unmovable courage to be exact, to effectively respond to the nefarious crisis that is impacting many black boys in public schools across the nation.

Dr. Walter Milton, Jr.

Often we find scores of black male students who exist on the edge of life. Many are faced with what appears to be insurmountable odds; they have been marginalized to the degree that they believe their options are very limited instead of limitless. It is apparent time and time again that schools and educators remind us that a high degree of black boys are in or on the brinks of being placed in special education. However, these same children are gifted in their life skills. The question then is how do we transport their home and community giftedness into the classroom?

Many educators have been psychologically and intellectually whipped into believing that these students automatically will remain in an abyss or a conundrum – the deficit model is vastly applied. The only way that educators can counteract this phenomenon is to go to the edge and stand with the students who are lingering on the edge and compassionately lead them toward the center. Most often, this takes a raw and unwavering courage.

One significant test of quality leadership is how well the leader copes with disappointments, defeats or some overriding adversity. Voltaire, in praising the Duke of Marlborough, called it, "Calm courage in the midst of tumult." It is going to take courage, unmovable courage to be exact, to effectively respond to the nefarious crisis that is impacting many black boys in public schools across the nation. We have to have a vision, and it must be sustainable whether in the midst of challenge or triumph.

I remember growing up in the inner city of Rochester, New York, and wondering how I was going to overcome my circumstances. I knew that I wanted to go to college; I also knew that if I had the opportunity to attend college, I would be the first person in my family to achieve this goal. Although neither of my parents graduated from high school, they instilled in me the expectation of excellence. My father was my driving force. Unlike so many fathers in my neighborhood who had abandoned their families, my father remained a constant in my life. He reminded me daily of the importance of hard work, the value of having a plan and the importance of embracing sacrifice.

Early in my career, I came to the firm conclusion that I wanted to become a school superintendent. This interest was sparked from the experiences I had in high school and college. Also, the backdrop of my desire was to make a deep and lasting impact in the lives of students, particularly black males mainly because I could identify with this population and knew the challenges that would await them.

I am the product of American public schools. As a result, I have always been led to believe that our society is one that encourages and appreciates the value of a quality education. It has been widely held that an education is a vital tool necessary for a thriving and forward moving citizenry. In other words, education is critical to society's survival and must be secured and protected. If this is true, it is vital that we place intentional focus on black males in America's schools.

It is my hope that we embrace the idea that all children can learn. Personally, I am dedicated to finding the means to ensure that this occurs in the spheres in which I can make the most significant contributions. The greatest divine gift given to humanity, aside from existence, is the ability to execute and affect future life. The sum total of future life is in fact the students who are entrusted to the care of educators. Our students represent humanity's hopes, dreams and aspirations. Every student, regardless of their social or economic circumstances, deserves the right to be educated in a nurturing and well-structured learning environment where they are encouraged to think freely, take chances and reach their full learning potential. If this is achieved, then our society's future is brighter because of the well-prepared, self-aware and self-determined adults who will hold the welfare of our society in their hands. As a result of this, I am compelled to shed light on what is happening to black male students in America's public schools.

We have to ensure that our schools are more than just a place for black males to go. Our schools must foster the successful growth of our boys' mental capabilities, social attitudes, emotional health, physical fitness, language proficiency, integrity and character. Black males have the right to a quality education.

Chapter Three

Looking Back
While Looking Ahead

*Offering help is one thing, but giving
hope is more important.*

Rex Deloney

High School Art Teacher

When posed with the question of "Why black men must save black boys in America's Public schools?" – I can only look back upon my experience as a student in the public school system. As I look back upon my twenty-two years in public education, my mind drifts back to how I ended up in the classroom today.

Ironically, before I ever exhaled or inhaled, I was in a classroom. My mother, a retired school - teacher was a substitute teacher while she was pregnant with me. So, I guess teaching was inbred in me. I was the seventh and final addition to the family of William Henry DeLoney, Jr. and Hazel B. DeLoney of North Little Rock, Arkansas. There were five boys and two girls. My father was a civil engineer, the community barber and a minister at our family church, Holy Temple Church of God in Christ. As already mentioned, my mother was an educator but also a talented seamstress, missionary and ardent worker in the church. My earliest memories of my childhood are drenched in the church. It seemed that everything that I learned or knew stemmed from the time spent on that corner at 1322 Pulaski Street in Little Rock, Arkansas.

As a child, I looked up to my four brothers, all of whom had varying degrees of artistic talent. Interestingly, I would become the only one to pursue a career in the arts. My brother William, Jr., or Henry as we called him, served as my first role model. Henry was an athlete, and it seemed that he could play any and every sport with ease. He was the first person that I can recall who took a true interest in my artistic ability. He would bring sports magazines and notebook paper home from high school so I could draw and paint. I thought he hung the moon and the stars, both visually and metaphorically! In today's society, many young men look up to the athletes and entertainment personalities they watch on television, but my role model was just down the hallway.

There were so many men that laid a strong foundation in my early years, and the beauty of it was that they all could be found in my family, neighborhood and church. My father instilled a strong work ethic in all of his sons, whether we embraced it or not. We did not have idle time as teenagers; it was always school, church or work. I grudgingly despised the fact that we were not allowed to do many of the things that our peers were doing back in the day but in hindsight, it is what made us the men we are today. My paternal grandfather, affectionately known as Big Daddy, taught me so many life lessons that helped mold my character as a young boy, and they are even more applicable today. I often refer to one of Big Daddy's lessons when I mentor my young men today. At the age of 13, he sat me down and told me, "You don't need to laugh and play around so much; a well-rounded man knows when and where to laugh, work and play."

In the Glenview, Illinois neighborhood where I grew up, I was surrounded; by black men; who were successful teachers, principals, coaches and college professors, as well as good husbands and fathers. These men all carried themselves in a way that made my peers and I aspire to walk in their shoes one day. It was rewarding to know that a casual walk through my neighborhood would provide a virtual tour of strong black men who were civic pillars in my town.

A teacher named Ken Dickson had the most profound effect on my life. Mr. Dickson was my high school art teacher at North Little Rock Northeast High School. He also taught art to a few of my older brothers during their high school years. For the first time in my public education, I had a teacher in my favorite subject matter that I had something in common with – we were both black. I immediately felt a comfort level and a sense of empowerment due to the fact that this man brought a cultural relevance to what I had aspired to be since a child. Mr. Dickson did more than teach me about art. I learned character, poise and integrity. Mr. Dickson saw something in me and shared life lessons with me that I have and will draw from for the rest of my career. I always was in awe of the way he was able to challenge me to grow as a student, artist and young man. His style was laid back but effective. I worked harder in Mr. Dickson's class than any other class in high school because I felt he could relate more to my position in life and because he had walked in my shoes as a young man. My high schools years were more memorable and meaningful because of the time I spent in Mr. Dickson's class.

I must admit that after graduating from high school my plans were to become a freelance sports illustrator and not a teacher! I enrolled at the University of Central Arkansas where I received a bachelor of arts degree in commercial art. After receiving my degree, I moved to the Pacific Northwest to a small city called Yakima, Washington. While there, I worked as a freelance artist in the field of my dreams, sports illustration. I enjoyed that lifestyle; however, the inconsistency of steady income became an issue. It was at that point that I started working as a paraprofessional in a high school just to make ends meet until I hit the big time in the art world.

One day, the art teacher at the high school saw some of my work and invited me to speak to his art class. After speaking to his class, he told me I should consider teaching art. I took his advice and within eighteen months, I was teaching middle school art. I taught, coached, worked in the community and mentored in the Yakima Valley for the next 15 years.

During that time, I was blessed to mentor and give back to many of the young black men in the community. Yakima was vastly different than my neighborhood back in North Little Rock. Many of the young men whom I worked with did not have a strong male role model or father figure in their lives. It was through teaching, coaching and my artwork that I was able to share my life lessons from my father, grandfather, neighbors and teachers to help mold and build their character. I noticed the same feeling of empowerment on many of their faces and in their attitudes that I experienced as a student in Mr. Dickson's class.

Teaching was an awesome responsibility that I had said I would never undertake; yet there I was with the future minds of society in my hands. Indeed, at times I felt like a brother from another planet as I began to work with the young men I encountered. There was a definite void in their self-esteem and self-worth. I knew it was because of the smaller minority population, and the even smaller percentage of professional black men for them to aspire to be like. I felt I had an obligation to give to them what was so freely given to me as a young man: life lessons from my father, wisdom from my grandfather, and the character and professional poise displayed by my mentor and teacher, Mr. Dickson.

I felt an overwhelming burden to ensure these young

men knew that they were capable of achieving lofty goals not previously considered. Offering help is one thing, but giving hope is more important. Hope allows one to believe that despite what they have been told or what they have seen, there still looms the possibility of measurable success. My goal was to provide opportunities in the classroom, on the field of competition and in the community, so other educators could see their worth and afford them the same efficacy that other students receive.

I spent my years in Yakima teaching, mentoring and nurturing a cadre of young men through their adolescence. I sensed a responsibility to do for them what had been done for me as a child. I always felt there were not enough black men in the classrooms for them to look up to or identify with, so I made it my passion to provide an outlet to address their ever growing concerns of self-worth and self-reliance.

My work within the school and community afforded me the opportunity to apply for and become the head football coach at the local high school where I had worked for five years. While my tenure as coach was short, God once again had allowed my position to be a source of pride and motivation for the young men I had mentored for so many years.

In 2004, I moved back to Arkansas after the death of my father. I worked one year in the Pulaski County School District before receiving my current position at Central High School where I serve as an art instructor, chair of the Fine Arts Department and co-sponsor of the Gentlemen Club. The club meets bi-weekly with a mission to provide positive motivation by fostering and facilitating a sincere respect for manhood while improving the future attitudes of young men through community service and educational excellence.

I closely monitor all of the members' grades and their behavior in school. Finally, and equally as important, I serve as liaison with the parents. The Gentlemen Club is open to male students who are willing to abide by the mission statement and guidelines.

Guest speakers are invited once a month to share words of inspiration with the young men. The young men attend educational field trips, perform community service and actively engage in student government. The most rewarding part of the club is that I can play a role in molding the character of young men during their most impressionable years.

I strongly feel that because of the erosion of the strong male role models in families and some communities, and the influx of societal ills affecting young black males, it is essential that black men save black boys in America's public schools. Teachers have the ability to affect eternity with their words, actions and beliefs. It can be daunting because what we do and how well we do it determines future generations. It is the relationship that matters most when working with impressionable young minds.

I only wanted to be an artist. Yet when I walked in that classroom some twenty years ago, I realized I had something worth sharing. Something that was ingrained in me.

Chapter Four

Endless Possibilities

I have come across an overwhelmingly large demographic of young black men who do not actually know where they are headed in life. With no plan and little motivation, the state of their developing manhood lays in the balance.

Milo Austin

Former Middle School Teacher
College and NFL Coach

As Dr. Martin Luther King, Jr. sat imprisoned in a jail cell in Birmingham, Alabama, in 1963, he penned his now famous "Letter from Birmingham Jail" in which he encouraged his disheartened followers and gave hope and inspiration to a nation by stating, "You must confront your shattered dream."

The dream of playing professional football shared by so many young black males in today's American society was something that I believed was truly within my reach. However, as I matriculated through high school and then on to college, that dream slowly began to crack. Despite my hard work, determination and commitment, the dream that had defined me for so long and shaped my life's path shattered. Confronting my shattered dream is what changed the direction of my life. Putting together the pieces of my previous hopes and dreams, and reshaping them into a more fulfilling and purposeful life's work is what brought me to the path that I am on today.

Though it was a brief period in my life, I distinctly can recall the days when my parents were together, married and living under one roof. At the age of five and the eldest of three children, my parents divorced and changed the makeup and structure of the family that my twin sisters and I had come to know. Love and family were always present in my upbringing, but the divorce took its toll on my childhood, and I ended up living in a multitude of households, including my mother's, grandparents' and finally my father's.

As often happens when there is only one parent to take care of the needs of a child, I fell victim to many negative influences and experiences outside the home. Being the product of a divorced home seemed quite normal to me at the time, and it is still an unfortunately common occurrence in our communities. The major difference between my situation and most others that I witnessed in my youth and continue to come across in my daily life is that my father has always been a vital, omnipresent and unwavering part of my life. Without any hesitation, I can call him my first and greatest role model. Ivan Wesley Austin was and currently is the hardest working and most honest, sincere and compassionate man I know. Through his actions and consistent display of devotion, a seed was planted within the makeup of my character that would remain with me throughout my journey and serve as a reminder of true manhood and maturity.

Even with a strong male presence in my life, I strayed far from the right path and found myself making many poor decisions as a young man. Like so many young black men do as they experience freedom and independence, I became attracted to the wrong things. I placed value in money and popularity, and lost my focus on academics, family and the morals I was taught as a child. At fourteen years of age as a high school freshman, I was arrested and charged with grand theft larceny. For months, a friend and I were involved in a money-making scheme we devised in which we would steal articles of clothing and compact discs and sell them to our peers for a one hundred percent profit.

The first time we decided to do it, my heart was racing and I could hear my conscience warning me loud and clear. The more we stole, the easier it got. Each time I broke the law, my once audible conscience was silenced a bit more. That attraction to easy money grew until our string of good luck came to a sudden and devastating halt. What had become second nature ended with two officers in plain clothes arresting us and placing us in the back of a police vehicle. My "friend" told the police that I forced him to be involved and subsequently was released into his parents' custody. Upon hearing of my criminal activity and resulting imprisonment, my father decided to purposely work an additional shift at his job in order to let me experience the full severity of my situation. That act and his simple statement, "I'm disappointed," impacted me greatly, but I still had so many life lessons to learn before I completely turned my life around and sought to make a difference on a larger scale.

I continued to go against the grain that my father sought to establish in my life, but the one thing that remained constant in my life was my father's unconditional love and unwavering commitment to me. An athletic scholarship to a premier private school in the Washington, D.C. area helped fuel my dreams of making it big in the sports arena. As I got older, my athletic abilities were celebrated at my school and sought after by colleges. Truancy and disinterest effectively killed my chances of attending college, athletic scholarship or not. I was ineligible to play at any major college or university due to my less than adequate high school record.

I found myself an athletically gifted and highly sought after senior with no prospects for the future due to my own actions and inactions. Crippled by my NCAA Clearinghouse rejection and a lack of guidance and information regarding collegiate sports, I ended up attending the only school that was willing to give me a chance. The Division III institution was not exactly what I had envisioned for myself. This was the first in a series of events that taught me about restructuring my dreams and rising to the challenges of my surroundings. Equipped with the short-term goal of playing at the most elite collegiate level, I worked hard both physically and academically and was able to transfer to West Virginia University after two years. Years before, my father had planted the seed of hard work and accountability within me by repeatedly telling me to "leave no doubt" in the minds of my coaches, teachers and teammates. It was simple – leave no doubt about your work ethic; leave no doubt about your commitment; and leave no doubt about your intentions to be the best.

I took that leave-no-doubt attitude with me to West Virginia and was able to earn a starting spot on a team that competed in the Gator Bowl during my first eligible year. I had put in the work and was beginning to realize the true possibility of my dreams, and it felt great to know that I had done this through my own efforts. Then, my senior football season happened. An injury-laden year brought me a torn hamstring before the start of the season. Following that, I sustained a broken leg and broken thumb, which effectively ended my chances of shining and achieving draft-worthy accolades. That season effectively shattered my dreams. I had placed so much of myself into becoming the athlete I had dreamed of being for so long. My career plans were wrapped up in that dream; my financial success was wrapped up in that dream; and my life's direction was wrapped up in that dream.

Upon graduating from college, I chose coaching as my desired career path. As a result of my deferred dreams, I had to come to grips with the reality of my situation, and I actively sought to direct my life in such a way that I could merge my passion for football and the life lessons I had experienced thus far. The objective on my first resume as a collegiate football coach candidate stated the following:

"I believe that the game of football is a microcosm of life. I feel my calling is to effect positive change in the lives of student-athletes using the avenue of football. The purpose of every young man that comes to college is to leave a better individual. My job as a coach is to aid in that process through providing quality leadership on and off the field. My life experiences coupled with my thirst for knowledge of football gives me the opportunity to be the best coach I can on any level."

At the time, I thought the words sounded good, but as I progressed in my career, this objective became my life's work.

I have been blessed to be a part of four outstanding universities and have worked diligently for their football programs. As a player, I was focused on "making it" and "getting paid," but as a coach I started to see the real need was for players to not just be athletes, but student-athletes. I saw the need for the development of these young men who trusted the football programs with their lives and futures. My own story taught me one certainty about the game of football: it is terminal. One day, the lights will go off on the field, the crowd will be gone and your jersey will be retired. At the end of all of that, there has to be more. There is a need for a path at the end of that dream.

My biggest success in life has been fully committing myself to my family and pledging a lifetime of partnership to my wife, who has been a driving force in helping me piece together my life in the wake of my broken dream. All of the lessons about the strength of family that my father taught me through his actions were made even clearer to me when I started my own family. As a coach, I had the opportunity to interview with Head Football Coach Brian Kelly of the University of Notre Dame, and he coined a term that stuck with me, "other centeredness."

Other centeredness is the concept of thinking of other people before you think of yourself and doing for others and functioning as a community rather than as an individual. I gained this sense of other centeredness first from my father, and then from my wife and daughter. I learned what it means to sacrifice and be committed and devoted. I developed unselfish dreams. I gained a greater sense of community and responsibility, and I began to look at life through a new perspective.

Other centeredness is something that is seemingly unnatural to our current generation of young men, particularly young black men. Because of all the negative issues that they face in the world, the armor of protection they have to wear has become thick and bulky to protect them from being continuously hurt. This heavy armor causes them to convey a negative vibe that often puts teachers, police officers and other men on guard.

Consequently, they always find themselves being targeted in class and in the community without truly understanding why.

My counterbalance to this problem is to use football to educate them about a multitude of life lessons. The first thing they must know is athletics, and specifically football, is not easy. If it were, everyone would be playing. Therefore, players have to realize that they are special. They are special because they are student-athletes, because they are part of a whole team and because they impact their school in a positive way. Secondly, I make a point of making sure that my players know that I will always be honest with them and have their best interest at heart. From there, the level of trust is elevated and mutual respect follows. Lastly, I mandate that each young man gets involved in as many community service projects as possible to instill a sense of other centeredness in them.

Putting all of these tenants into action brings about actual change on and off the field. Impacting these student-athletes by developing them as whole individuals will pay dividends far into the future. Providing them with tools to grow as men is what will make a difference in their lives.

While on the university level, I saw a need for guiding and refocusing for the black student-athletes. I always felt that if the young men I coached could have been inspired at an earlier age, they could arrive at college prepared and locked in to the task at hand.

A desire to be close to my family brought me out of collegiate sports and onto the high school football and education path. My reconstructed dream is now one that is unselfish. When I look in the mirror, I now see countless, nameless youthful faces over my shoulder whose growth and development I charge myself with impacting.

As I have transitioned into my new career path in the public school system, I have come across an overwhelmingly large demographic of young black men who do not actually know where they are headed in life. With no plan and little motivation, the state of their developing manhood lays in the balance. I feel like athletics can serve as an excellent conduit for disseminating the information they need in order to be vital contributors to their communities. And in order to do so, I, like my father, must be consistent with and supportive of them from the very beginning.

If used correctly, athletics can be the cornerstone of a young man's life, providing him not only with stability he may be lacking in his life, but also by instilling a sense of accountability and community. In team sports, you must think of someone other than yourself and, if you fail to do your job, the whole team will suffer as a result. Ultimately, my goal is to use any sports program of which I am a part as a coach/educator/mentor to internally develop a sense of purpose in these young men. The athletics aspect of it all will push them to become mentally tough and aware of the impact of a team. They will learn to work toward a goal and be accountable for their ability to overcome adversity.

Off the field, which is most important, I will cover five

areas for the young men: life skills, continuing education, community involvement, career discovery and character development. Through these five components, the young men will be challenged to become better men, citizens, future fathers and husbands. Well after their playing days are over, the knowledge acquired from this program will stick with them and become building blocks that shape the principles by which these young men live.

There is a quote that puts my life's work in perspective, and it says, "A man should never stand alone, unless he is taking a stand." For the next generation of black men coming through the public school system, I am willing to stand-alone.

Chapter Five

Always Strive for Excellence

I think one has to always remember that as a racial equity leader there are going to be times that you will grow weary in this struggle and have to dig deep to keep on keeping on.

Dr. Charles L. Hopson (1960-2012)

Former Superintendent of Schools

We start saving black boys by first acknowledging that a problem exists with race. The challenges for me in my former role as superintendent of the Pulaski County Special School District in Little Rock, Arkansas, actually differed very little from those I experienced growing up in this state during the desegregation of schools in the early 1960s.

In theory, the intent of desegregation efforts all across this country was to address systemic educational inequities in public schools. In practice, I find myself often questioning whether this country ever really was committed in practice to the true purpose of desegregation when I witness many of the gross systemic inequities that not only still exist in my current and past school districts, but in districts all across this country. Have we simply been giving lip service to truly eliminating racial academic disparity and systemic inequities in our public schools across this country through desegregation efforts since Brown vs. the Board of Education? Do we really have the will and courage as a country to confront the core of racial inequities in our schools? Or, do we simply continue to languish in the comfort and rewards of business as usual and live in an illusion of perpetual denial that acclaims, "I do not see race"?

It is the above paradox that has provided the greatest frustration and challenge for me as a racial equity leader during my tenure and career in moving from theory to practice. I recall my early experiences as a student at McRae Elementary School when my parents enrolled me in the segregated school system of the South that existed in Prescott, Arkansas. My father was a Marine and my kindergarten year had been spent on a base with integrated classrooms in Quantico, Virginia, prior to us moving back to Arkansas. As I think back now, attending this segregated school was the initial building block to establishing the powerful systemic counter-narrative that drives my passion as a racial equity leader, even though I initially attended the integrated kindergarten class on the military base where my race was essentially invisible or nonexistent to me.

I entered a world at McRae Elementary where everyone around me had my skin color. I recall looking out the window during the afternoon in awe and with pride as I saw the band in majestic purple and gold swaying and dancing in formation as they played the popular tune at that time I now know as "The Horse." Many of us daydreamed about one day being high school students as we watched them outside of our elementary classroom windows.

In the classroom, the pedagogical message that provided the thrust for my current counter-narrative paradigm as a racial equity leader was the recurring message that "we had to be twice as good, we had to study twice as hard." This theme was common from every teacher at McRae Elementary in both overt and covert actions. At that time in my life, I did not have the intellectual capacity to understand that the faculty and staff at McRae were creating a powerful counter-narrative within each of us that would be transformational in my future as I matured as a racial equity leader. The one thing teachers in segregated schools had in common with us as students was that they had first-hand experience with the ugly and deadly stings of institutional racism and the racial norms of inferiority that created the foundation of systemic inequity.

I have come to understand in my maturity that the illusion or lie surrounding racial achievement disparity or the so-called achievement gap has focused on addressing false assumptions of deficiency aimed at "fixing the student" so that they fit the cognitive or psychological model of the middle class, male white student. As a racial equity leader, the anger becomes rage as I see school districts across this country treat the widening academic disparity of black students and their failure in public schools as if it were the result of their intellectual deficiency. This is a lie from the pits of Hell.

I feel so blessed to have had the foundation of my educational experience shaped in that rural, segregated elementary school. It helped me survive integration, which was nothing more than the assimilation and acculturation to the racial norms of the white school in our city. The majestic purple and gold of McRae became the maroon and white of the white school; our mighty, mighty tiger became a wolf; and everything that once symbolized the proud traditions of our powerful counter-narrative was either marginalized or completely removed from our educational experience, including the scattering or demotion of McRae teachers and administrators. Integration was complete. What once mattered to our sense of identity as children of African descent was now defined by the psychological narrative norms of the white school.

The greatest single challenge I face as a racial equity leader in moving from theory to practice is the dueling tensions in creating the counter-narrative that once existed in the classrooms of McRae Elementary to challenge the powerful systemic constructs of a dominant white narrative in our public schools. The dominant narrative is so entrenched and institutionalized by status quo or business as usual that it presents a constant threat to career security and opens you to scrutiny and attack when it is challenged by either word or actions. The most difficult thing for me to witness is the fear of some black educators who have embraced the dominance of the majority narrative through acculturation or assimilation for the rewards it offers, and they shy away from providing the culturally affirming counter-narrative because of the risk of punishment. It is the systemic control of the dominant narrative that exerts the forces of both covert and overt institutional racism to counter my efforts as a racial equity leader.

I have come to accept my role as an educational leader in this area to be one of alienation and isolation. As a racial equity leader, I find that I often am viewed as radical or different, and some are guarded in their association with me or my practices as I attempt to be a transformational leader. I remember so vividly as a high school principal leading this work in a Portland, Oregon, high school and being constantly reminded about the tremendous risk or danger to my career if I fell from this tight rope without a safety net from the system. I have come to understand that the fear that is created by the dominance of the majority narrative is a part of my battle in walking the talk. While I have overcome the fear that once paralyzed and stifled me as a racial equity leader, I now have to constantly be sensitive to the fear that exists within both the dominant narrative and the new counter-narrative through courageous transformational equity leadership.

The dominant context fears what it does not fully know

or understand, while the new counter-narrative that we seek to create as racial equity leaders is fearful of retribution or lack of acceptance from the majority status quo. This work is not for the faint of heart. It requires a passion, conviction and courage to be comfortable with not fitting in or having others around you not feel comfortable because you never shy away from constantly keeping that uncomfortable topic of race front and center.

I think one has to always remember that as a racial equity leader there are going to be times that you will grow weary in this struggle and have to dig deep to keep on keeping on. I remember being a top finalist for the superintendent of schools in St. Paul Public Schools in Minnesota, and I was worn down from back-to-back meetings and faced a crowd of about three hundred citizens in a community forum who were disgruntled about the wide achievement gap in that school district, particularly between black and white students. I hosted questions from the crowd and talked very candid and open about the challenges of the achievement gap and the fact that we honestly have to confront and isolate the issue of race. When the session was over, I was drained and felt such a sense of hopelessness from the crowd and their outrage over academic disparity. I found myself asking the question presented to Ezekiel in the Bible when he was set down in the midst of the valley, which was full of dry bones, and God said, "Son of Man, can these bones live?" Can the dry bones of eliminating academic racial disparity and systemic inequity really live in this country, which is so comfortable with the illusion and lies of the powerful status quo? The question perplexed me as I boarded the plane the next day to meet a group of principals from Portland in Washington, D.C.

While in Washington, D.C., the group asked me to join them for a tour of Arlington National Cemetery. I still was grappling with the weight of the question about truly eliminating academic disparity and was feeling too discouraged with my philosophical struggle to go anywhere. But, I remembered how Ezekiel persevered anyway in his dry bones moment, and I joined the group that day. We boarded the guided tour tram and as it turned a corner in the historic cemetery, I caught a glimpse of the headstone of Thurgood Marshall. I immediately told the group that I needed to get off so I could walk over to a monument. I quickly made my way to the headstone of Judge Thurgood Marshall, and I stood in silence as I attempted to reconcile my perplexing question. While standing at his grave site, I pondered whether Judge Marshall would have predicted, or even envisioned, that more than fifty years after Brown vs. the Board of Education that desegregation efforts to create systemic equity would fail so miserably in this country for black children. Many of these black children still experience an inequity of facilities and resources by virtue of concentrated race and poverty designed as a result of systemic neighborhood practices. As I stood lost in thought, a principal walked up to me and asked for my thoughts. I replied, "Do you think Judge Marshall would have anticipated after the Brown decision that black children in most urban school systems are in many instances worse off than they were before the Brown decision?" As I asked that question, I received my answer just as God said to Ezekiel, "Behold, I will cause breath to enter into you, and ye shall live."

My doubts were gone and my conviction once again affirmed. My purpose in this work as a racial equity leader must be to cause theory to become breath that enters a counter-narrative to combat the dominant dry bones narrative of systemic inequity and achievement disparity so that practice ultimately creates a culture for racial equity to live.

Chapter Six

"We Must Overcome"

I was simply told, and I will never forget, "You are not college material, and I recommend that you follow in your dad's footsteps."

Dr. T.C. Wallace, Jr.

My story is one of beating the odds and making education a priority that took me from the streets of Gary, Indiana to serving as a superintendent for several major school districts across the country.

I grew up in one of the toughest urban school districts and cities in the United States – Gary, Indiana. I had a hard-working dad and a supportive mom who was the stabilizing force in my life and that of my only sister. My dad worked in the heat of the steel mills for over thirty years, and my mom was a domestic engineer who provided the stability in our lives and made certain that education was among our priorities.

My dad had a sixth grade education and my mom was fortunate enough to complete eleven years of education, but possessed what we commonly call in urban school settings, "mother wit." She certainly was a pillar of strength for me as I grew up, and matriculated from Gary, Indiana through undergraduate school at Central State University in Wilberforce, Ohio and then onto a Big Ten university, Indiana University, for both my masters and my doctorate degrees.

Indeed, I am an example of a product coming out of a tough urban school district and reaching heights never imagined during my youth or the lives of my parents. There were many who were involved throughout the years in helping me maintain the appropriate focus through stern mentorship and guidance that enabled me to carve out a path that has led me to where I am today as an urban school superintendent.

At the age of twelve, I was very much involved in neighborhood athletics, which were formalized by my first African American mentor and coach as a participant in the "Biddy Basketball" program. Coach D led us to a state basketball championship, which launched a very active athletic career for me in multiple sports. This ultimately began the road that I had traveled from the streets of Gary, Indiana to Central State University.

The second significant African American mentor was my high school football coach who guided myself, and others through our high school athletic years and created the opportunity to move into higher education. These two

African American role models are just examples of individuals instrumental in my life that I constantly reflect upon when I look back on my career.

Let me digress a moment to my unfortunate experience as a tenth grader, when I was exposed to cultural bias and racism that was prevalent then and on some level, still exists today in public education. As with many of us, my high school counselor purported to lay out my career path, set my direction and determine my destiny. That path was one of following in the footsteps of my dad working in the Gary steel mills as opposed to pursuing education after high school. I was simply told, and I will never forget, "You are not college material, and I recommend that you follow in your dad's footsteps."

I was disappointed. I was hurt, and I was angry that someone who did not know me, who did not understand my culture and background, who did not understand what I had to endure growing up in the streets of Gary, Indiana would dare try to determine my destiny. However, those words as harsh as they may have seemed laid the foundation for my motivation and commitment to be guided by my African American mentors and role models. They instilled a belief in me that I could become whatever it was that I chose to become. Thus, it was truly a blessing in disguise. It helped me further define my own destiny, defining who I was, what I wanted in life, and what I was willing to do to accomplish my dreams and not carry out the expectation of someone else. I thank my mentors along the way for their wisdom and guidance.

I was fortunate in that I had some level of athletic capabilities and I found that my skills were such that I could be successful in athletics. In that regard, my mentors who provided mentorship during my secondary school experience effectively channeled me into higher education, when I accepted a scholarship to participate in football at Central State University. I continue to be grateful that Coach D and Coach B, as they were commonly called, took me under their wings and helped me matriculate from the streets of Gary, Indiana to the campus of Central State University. My career as an educator began and athletics became my secondary focus.

I realized and set my sights on becoming a teacher/educator accepting the fact that my chances of a professional football career were limited. It was in that vein that I became serious about education, majored in elementary education, obtained a bachelor's degree and began my career as a teacher in, as you might guess, my home city of Gary, Indiana.

I began teaching at the elementary level, moved to the middle school level and ultimately was asked by a Caucasian male – the third individual instrumental in my life – my principal Mr. H., to consider administration. At his urging, I completed the coursework necessary to become an administrator and began my career as an elementary principal. I worked very hard but knew this was just the beginning as I set my sights high. I wanted to become the best administrator that I could become and ascend one day to become a superintendent.

Along the way, I continued to be supported by various

mentors at various levels as I moved from principal to central office administrator to assistant superintendent and ultimately to the superintendent position in 1986.

I would say to those aspiring to educate young black males is there must be a significant adult in the life of every African American male, either within the home or outside of the home. We must have parents or other role models who are willing to step up and become collaborative partners in our lives for we know that we will experience adversity, and that we will have to overcome many challenges and obstacles along the way.

I have overcome numerous challenges, crossed over many obstacles to ascend to where I am today. Although the odds at times seemed to be stacked against me, it was my personal drive, dedication and determination that carried me through every step and every level along the way. I was convinced my attitude would determine my altitude. I had big dreams. I set my sights high. I possessed a strong work ethic and was willing to do whatever was necessary to be successful. I set the conditions for my destiny – that is, I set the conditions to be successful or to be a failure. For me, failure was not an option.

Let me share with you just one of my greatest challenges, which was in pursuing my doctorate degree from Indiana University, which is certainly the credential necessary to become a superintendent of schools. I applied to be admitted to the Department of School Administration at Indiana University in 1972. At that time, there had only been three African

American males who had been successful in completing the requirements for a doctorate in school administration. The University did not accept my application as it was submitted, but in fact, I was admitted to the Department of Urban Studies to which I had not applied. I did not take the news well. It was not what I had requested. It was not the direction that I wanted to pursue so without any parental support or mentorship, I took on the Department of Administration at Indiana University personally.

I drafted a hand-written, six-page letter, which I addressed to the then President Ryan at Indiana University, laying out my situation, my aspirations and my request for admission into school administration. I supported my argument by presenting to him a perfect 4.0 grade point average during my time at Indiana University. I also presented other professional successes in my aspirations to become a superintendent needing that doctoral degree to be maximally qualified.

I am pleased to share with you that President Ryan invited me to Indiana University, face-to-face, to plead my case for admission into the Department of School Administration. I accepted his invitation and promptly met with him. He concluded our session, which lasted about an hour, saying that I would be hearing from him in the next few days with a final determination. I returned to Gary, where I awaited President Ryan's response, and within a matter of days I received his response indicating that I had been admitted into the Department of School Administration for further work on my doctorate at Indiana University.

That was the first major obstacle or challenge in my quest to become a superintendent of schools. I then went on to complete my course work and my dissertation and be granted a doctorate degree in education in 1979. I was then qualified for the highest-level position in the education arena. Strategically, I then moved into positions from being a principal to becoming a director of human resources, assistant superintendent of human resources, and ultimately superintendent in 1986.

Today, I am pleased to say that for the past twenty-five years I have served as a superintendent of schools in districts such as Saginaw-Buena Vista, Michigan; Jackson Mississippi; Roosevelt, New York; Mount Clemens, Michigan; and Lansing School District in Lansing, Michigan.

My career has fulfilled my objectives going back some forty-five years to become the very best educator that I could become and ascending to a superintendent in public education. My story is just one that indicates that every youngster has the capacity to dream big, work hard, and never lose focus on his or her goal.

As the Reverend Jesse Jackson said many, many years ago, "If you can conceive it, and you believe it, you can achieve it."

This is my story of how one youngster from Gary, Indiana who grew up in poverty went on to become a Superintendent of Schools, a position held for some 25 years. I thank my family, my coaches, my mentors along the way for believing in me and helping me fulfill my dreams.

My work now consists of promoting, assisting and mentoring other African American males in fulfilling their dreams to rise from poverty and above adversity, to stand tall, set goals and work hard to be committed to accomplishing his or her goals to become the best that they can become.

Chapter Seven

This is One Fight We Simply Cannot Afford to Lose

... Being a male is a matter of gender;
being a man is a matter of responsibility.

Larry Hemingway, Sr.

Alternative School Educator

Born in Chicago, Illinois on the city's south side on a Friday during a leap year can be a rather revealing test for a petite mother having her first child with her husband. While understanding that my mother graduated from high school through adversity and challenges, she decided a few years later to embrace the idea of living in another city to raise a family. In fact, growing up with a single parent in the home was one of a few silent assassins I dealt with as an African

American boy. I was raised in a single parent home because my mother chose to leave an abusive relationship with my father who is now on pace to being out of the picture for the next twenty-plus years of my life. There were a total of six of us growing up and I, being the eldest, took on more responsibility seemingly by nature.

The desire to be successful was a yearning that didn't often find its way to the forefront of the minds of my peers, church members and school faculty who didn't look like me. My mother, who stood in unwavering faith, appeared to be always caught with a smile even in the toughest of life's storms. She would always find a way to water my garden with gratitude. It was and has always been easy as the eldest child of my mother's kids to accept responsibility as opposed to running from it – even though running from responsibility was what seemed to have encamped around my neighborhood.

The strong-willed women of my house often bore the heavy burden of sacrifice, lack, and yet had the ability to deposit into my emotional savings account so that I could one day begin to draw down upon it and share it with others.

"And let us not be weary in well doing: for in due season we shall reap, if we faint not." Galatians 6:9

This tidbit of wisdom and biblical text would find its way into our Christian home for reassurance that we would be alright. Discouragement is an ongoing tool of an enemy. In fact, there were times during my adolescent years where questions surrounding being a man or not being a man was not always about what it seemed. For the most part, there has always been a strong foundation and a sense of approval while remaining focused on making a difference. I began to develop a sense of hope on my own that started to shape my outlook on life alongside the new attitude I was developing. Being taught throughout my adolescent years how to trust in God and not lean on my own understanding made sense to an enthusiastic African American boy with a balance of two worlds. I had to balance being poor and being exposed to a steady Christian upbringing while living in a community surrounded by drugs, gangs and alcohol.

I acquired a sense of the big picture and thus strived to learn from all my experiences both positive and negative. With the tool of a public school house, I was able to buckle down and obtain my high school diploma while inadvertently beating the odds that were against me. In fact, one school staff member whom I listened to closely for advice and insight during my journey always said, "…we've gotten ours, you'd better get yours…" With this being said, I gained insight from a variety of people collectively: people in the educational systems, churches, social service agencies, and even people in my neighborhood. There wasn't always positive communication that engulfed my humble, hungered and attentive ears, but there was always a message taken from circumstances. I realized that adding value to others had a great reward toward living rather than being selfish, thus continuing to ignite the philosophy of collective responsibility. This responsibility has continued to grow through desires to help other people. Being solution-oriented seemed like the ideal thing to look for especially since possibilities in every situation started with ideas.

Affirmations have helped me to get through tough times. While attending college right before getting married at the tender age of twenty-two, I realized that speaking things into existence had become a part of living that helped change the way things were received. Imagine hearing mentors and other people of collective influence begin to share with the masses that by reaffirming oneself and speaking positivity into everyday life situations, one could change the course of that which is desired. This new wave was something that challenged me in operating in the norm. The very breath of new life was pepper-minted into every ounce of my being. There is not a time that goes by where I do not celebrate the small victories that became enormous victories. This celebration wasn't alone. This celebration has always found its way into the arms of every well wisher, mentor, educator, parent, student, business professional, motivational speaker, life coach, therapist, technician, transformed thug, renewed hustler, sober ex-addict, and the list goes on and on. I have had high self-esteem that has warranted me to never feel ashamed, embarrassed or worthless. On the same coin, I've always felt responsible for what I can learn and give back.

Borrowing from the wisdom of African American males whom I assisted in my journey makes me an identity thief.

Allow me to explain. I have taken pieces of knowledge from each and every African American male that has been part of my life in short and long term, and even in absence. I've been able to receive collectively from them all. Call it selfishness, call it smart, or you can simply call it a collective responsibility being sifted. Being committed to helping African American males is something that will grow in history as an opportunity paved for kings to redirect kings toward their purpose while listening to destiny's brave stance to eliminate the lack of African American male willingness to be responsible. Some people ask me why I am committed to the work that I do and not focus on other areas that I can potentially be well off financially. My simple words to them are, "I love what I do; and besides, being a male is a matter of gender; being a man is a matter of responsibility."

Chapter Eight

Man Down

Because there are so many "men down,"
I am going to "man up."

Henry Kleckley

Middle School Language Arts Teacher

When he is born, a female nurse cleans him, feeds him and nurtures him for the first few days of his life. After a few days, he is ready to go home. His father disappeared as soon as he heard the words, "I am pregnant," so he has never been and never will be in the picture, except for maybe a child support check every month. So, this leaves his mother and his grandmother to raise him. In daycare, he is under the watchful eye and the care of a female nursery worker. The only males he sees in daycare are the bus drivers and maintenance workers.

When he makes it to elementary school, the principal, cafeteria workers, secretaries, nurses, librarians and, most importantly, teachers are all female. The one man in the elementary school is a custodian. In church, the pastor is male, but he does not have a tangible influence on the boy's life because the pastor is too busy and distant, and his Sunday school teacher, his children's pastor and his choir director are all female. He tries to play sports because his mom wants him to "toughen up," but he finds that sports are not his "cup of tea." He would much rather read a book or play an instrument.

Everything may seem right but once he hits middle school, seemingly out of nowhere, the underlying bitterness, anger and emptiness boil over into fits of rage, blatant disrespect and a total misplacement of priorities. He is desperately searching. He does not know that he needs a credible male voice because, after all, you cannot miss what you have never had. So he searches. He tries to find it in females but as soon as one makes him mad, it is on to the next. He keeps on searching. He tries to find it in friends, but no one seems to understand him. Still he searches. And while he is on this treasure hunt to fulfill his soul, time keeps moving and fundamental skills, both academically and socially, keep slipping away. He does just enough to pass, but he is at risk – at risk of becoming and creating another statistic. His mother and grandmother do not know what has happened to their "baby," and therein lays the rub. The whole time they have been calling him "baby," and they forgot they were raising a man. Now, he is growing up to be a "man down."

The expression, "man down," originated during combat. Whenever a fellow soldier was shot or injured during battle, his cohorts would shout, "Man down!" Then, fellow soldiers would retrieve the wounded, take them to safety and, if possible, patch them up to get ready for battle again. Well, this analogy rings true with our young black men in America. We currently are raising a generation of men who are…"man down!" *Man Down!* The number one cause of death among black men is homicide. *Man Down!* Black men in America make up sixty percent of the prison population and only four percent of the college population. *Man Down!* The average life span of a black man is 69.5 years, as opposed to an average life span of seventy-six years for the rest of America. *Man Down!* Seven out of ten African American households are headed by single mothers. *Man Down!* Black men are more than twice as likely to be unemployed as white men, leaving them more susceptible to crime and prison. *Man Down!* Nearly sixty percent of African American males drop out of high school.

Those are very sobering statistics. As an educator of young people for over thirteen years, I am on the frontlines every day and sadly, even as a black man, my most underachieving demographic in the classroom is black males. So, what do we do as a society? How do we raise up a fatherless generation?

Being raised in a single parent home, I know what it is like to live a life "behind the eight ball." Like most young men, I was raised in a home where the only credible, authoritative voices were that of my mom, grandma and aunt. In my home, my grandmother had five grandchildren sired by five different men. So, what changed in my life? How was I able to beat the statistics by graduating from college, getting married before raising a family, becoming a teacher and creating a new normal for my generation?

It was because God graced me to have a series of black men enter my life and show me a better way. Because of the influence of these men, I decided to become a youth pastor and teacher so I can have the same impression and influence on young people. When those men in my life saw me as a "man down," they decided to "man up" and do something about it. And that is my life's mantra. Because there are so many "men down," I am going to "man up." Young black men have plenty of guides and voices that are directing them toward destruction, but I have decided to be that credible voice in their ears and hearts. I have decided to let them know that they can, as young men, live life the right way and still have plenty of swag. I have decided to show young black men a new normal – a normal where we can flip the statistics one man at a time.

When soldiers see a man down, it takes great strength, determination and courage to help them. They literally have to "man up." That is what we as educators and mentors need to do for our young men. We need to "man up."

I found that young black men often respond positively to a black man's voice. However, with today's culture, respect is not automatically given – respect is earned. So, the first thing I do when I encounter any young black man is show them respect. I respect them by carrying myself in a respectful manner, dressing professionally, speaking professionally and treating them professionally. When they make bad decisions, I do not yell, cuss or belittle them; instead, I show them a better way. The language I speak is always positive. Most of the young black men today have not witnessed respect properly modeled for them. They see respect as fear. But if fear was respect, then it would not be called respect. So that is the first thing I do.

As an educator, the second thing I do for young black students is make my subject, language arts, relevant. Whenever we encounter new subject matter, I break it down into a language they can understand and concepts to which they can relate. I make sure we read literature written by authors who look like them and write about relatable characters. I also show them the benefits of the new knowledge by modeling it in my life and sharing stories with them about how the information helps me. Another thing I do is complete the work with them. If I assign a poem, I write a poem with them. If I assign an essay, I write an essay with them. Many of our young men have never seen a black man write a poem or give a speech. When they see me do it, they are inspired to do it as well.

The last thing I do for young black men is challenge them in a rigorous atmosphere. In my classroom, we are constantly pushing the envelope. If the curriculum requires a five-paragraph essay, we write a three- to five-page research paper. If the curriculum requires we read one book per nine weeks, we read three. We are always thinking, creating, inferring and challenging. The fact that we are Black marks with us with two strikes, so we have to be twice as good to beat out the next man. Besides, once young black men are bored, that is when they begin to cause the most trouble in the classroom. Young black men are never bored in my classroom because once you finish one task, there is always something else that can be done.

These three things – relationship, relevance and rigor – drive the instruction in my classroom and because of that, I have only written five office referrals in five years of teaching, and I have not written any office referrals in the last three years. Students perform well in class and have performed well on standardized tests. My methods are not one hundred percent foolproof but then again, the only thing in life that is one hundred percent is that nothing is one hundred percent. The bottom line is that most of my young black males are achieving in a world where most young black males do not achieve. And they are better men because of it.

In a society where most black males are "men down," there are a group of men that are willing to "man up." These men are taking responsibility for this fatherless generation, and they will take their heads out of the proverbial sand in order to create new norms in our culture. The future is bright for young black men and if each man reaches out to a man, we will slowly, but surely see those statistics turn for the better.

Chapter Nine

The Presence of a Man

What I have come to realize is that when there is no real leader or mentor, our youth tend to seek guidance from other sources that can negatively impact them.

Minister Duane Clayton

High School Assistant Principal

As a young black male, I can vividly remember matching the intelligence of my fellow classmates. In fact, many times I recall surpassing my peers' knowledge levels. My mother expected me to do well in school, and I did. Though this brief story may seem like a paradox, it is my fraction of time.

I grew up in a small town of 10,000 people near the Louisiana state line. In my early childhood, I can recall several of my teachers. During the preschool years my instructor was Mrs. Griffin; second grade, Mrs. Richards; third grade, Ms. Shapley; fourth grade, Mrs. Robinson; fifth grade, Mrs.

Atteberry; and sixth grade, Mrs. Montgomery. I had my first encounter with a black male teacher when I took an eighth grade civics class with Mr. Bobbie Anderson. He was the first major male influence in my life. Imagine how detrimental it can be for black male students to not have a positive black role model today? How might this scenario affect someone? Picture a black boy not having a father or a mentor to engage with and share much-needed times of bonding. This is not racial bias, because all young men need positive role models. What I have come to realize is that when there is no real leader or mentor, our youth tend to seek guidance from other sources that can negatively impact them. In fact, having no strong, positive male role models until eighth grade can be a matter of life and death.

Throughout school, I never struggled. Not at all. I was the kid that every teacher enjoyed having in their classes. It just so happened that my mother's occupation was that of a high school Social Studies teacher in a neighboring school district. Consequently, my mother's expectations of me where quite simple: Go to school and do what you are supposed to do. Secondly, I was always told to go and ask questions about anything that I did not understand. Finally, I was to act as if I had sense because my mother stated, "I did not raise any fools or dummies."

Throughout high school, I always maintained honor roll status. I can honestly say that in high school, I encountered teachers who added value to my being. It did not matter about their ethnicity or gender. The crux of me being able to succeed and digest information in school and hurdle potential obstacles came from an outstanding superwoman figure of my mother and fatherly figures of my grandfather and uncles.

Yet, when I ventured to college, it seemed as if I was a magnet for trouble. I knew that I had a purpose and destiny, but I did not know how to get to it. Being that I did not have my biological father around, I had a stepfather who was around through my senior year of high school. I did not meet my real pops until I was 18 years old. Without question, I really respected my stepfather because though he raised me as a bastard child, at least he was present. As time passed, I learned that my stepfather did not know his father because he died when he too was a young man. As a result, I experienced him raising me passively. I saw him get up and go to work. He balanced bills, he brought home some bacon, but he did not intentionally communicate with me. Looking through my dull lens, I figured that the frustration of not having a father fostered doubt and fear in my stepfather. I was not reared in a manner that I saw other kids' fathers raising them and spending time with them. I cannot recall ever going on a fishing trip with my dad. Recollecting a hunting weekend at a deer camp never comes to the forefront of my mind. This experience truly hurt me even though I denied the effects time and time again. Now that I am an adult, I realize that hurt people hurt other people. Consequently, I do not hold any ill will or wrong against my stepfather.

Today, as I jog down memory lane because I do not want to stay there, I visualize a plethora of actions and events that let me know that I escaped the hood. During my college years, I struggled financially because I had not been taught to manage money in a family setting. Foolishly, I wasted grant money and scholarship money. I had two academic scholarships that paid tuition, and room and board. My ignorance led me to purchase clothing with my leftover money instead of saving it. I had a daughter out of wedlock. As I continued to operate with a lack of wisdom, I began drinking and hanging out. Suddenly like commonplace, I was purchasing alcohol and drinking it. The drinking became habitual. Within months, I found myself in the dean's office and later the president's office facing suspension from school. "If it does not work out for you, young man, you can always go to work at McDonalds," the president of the institution stated. I let myself down as well as my football coach, teammates and family.

I found myself seeking admissions into other schools. I was accepted into another school in a larger city of Little Rock, Arkansas. Feeling as if I had a new lease on life, I gladly attended UALR. At UALR, I did not change my addictive behaviors of drinking and smoking. During my one semester stay at UALR, I lost one of my academic scholarships, and acquired a deeper dependency for alcohol and drugs. People wondered what I was doing. I had lost control of my life. How does this happen? Quite simple, I must say. I was traveling the Right Road and turned onto Agony Avenue.

At this point in my life, I was not oblivious to walking circumspectly, as the Bible tells Christians to do. However, I had book knowledge of the Bible, but not a zeal for God, Jehovah. During this transitional period in my life, I noticed that negative, seductive spirits were controlling me. When I finally hit my wit's end, my "Aha! Moment" manifested. I had experienced just about every detestable thing that a human could. If real talk means anything, I had graduated from the School of Hard Knocks. I was fluent in the lifestyle of thuggin.' One day, I had a Damascus Road experience when I realized that I was kicking against the pricks for what God's purpose was for my life. When I realized that I must live a purpose-driven life, I began to walk in a new area of life and liberty that was foreign to me.

For the last eleven years, I have dedicated myself to service, first of all to God. This freewill choice that I made allowed me to be able to access a power that I have never known. I began to be empowered to recognize and discern when students were facing challenges. **Romans 12: 1-2** became paramount in my life: *"If we do not sacrifice big, the return will not be great."* Dr. Mr. Luther King, Jr. sacrificed big and that cost him his life. We learned that without struggle there is no progress. One of the biggest contributions that adults, coaches, and educators can make with children is that we can love the lives of people enough to deny our own selfish desires. This servant attitude causes us to be able to say, we are first of all, servants of all, and we shall transcend all. Looking beyond the plateau popularity, we must go against the grain to educate other black boys about knowing who they are and their true identity. They must understand that we must not just go through struggles, but we must *grow through.*

We must educate them and celebrate them. We must be able to commend them for their acts of righteousness because they get so much negative reinforcement from shot callers and players in the hood.

It is very difficult to be an influence on young boys as we try to educate them and pour knowledge into them when they view our words of wisdom as dung because they see money and possessions as their measuring sticks for success and prosperity. The reason they scoff at our jewels of wisdom is because they can make more money in one week hustling in the dope game than we make over a month's time. While they enjoy the benefits and perks that come with hustling, they relish at the fact that the OGs (original gangsters) of the hoods give them props for their neighborhood clout and status. Our young boys feel more inclined to look up to rap artists like Young Jeezy, Rick Ross, Lil Wayne and Drake.

The systematic ignorance has to be eradicated in our homes, schools and athletic playing fields. For too long, these young men have been exploited for dunking basketballs and running touchdowns, and are strategically placed in special education to be safely promoted to the next grade level. When a young black male uses proper grammar, his neighborhood peers tell him, "You are acting white." More and more homes have single parent mothers raising these boys to be physically strong and intellectually weak. The problem is not only the absence of men as fathers but also the presence of passive men not protecting the future prodigy of the community.

Until we as men stop the unfavorable cycles that our fathers and mothers fostered for a fearful future, we shall have paralyzing predicaments that prevent our progress. You and I are the cycle breakers. Fredrick Douglass states that, "It is easier to build strong children than to repair broken men." Even though it may be easier to build strong boys, God is able to repair broken men. He restored David, Peter and Saul. And guess who else? He restored me.

More important than anything else stated is this: Acts 1:8 reads that *"Ye shall receive power after the Holy Spirit has come upon us and ye shall be a witness unto me in all the world."* The power is to share the good news with others. The power eliminates fear (false evidence appearing real). The beauty of this power explained in Acts Chapter 1 exemplified how the same message can impact the world. If we operate in genuine love and compassion, we can reach the masses. In closing, we should not just consider ourselves as teachers, but we shall consider ourselves as preachers!

How have I attempted to give back and live out my purpose so that young black males may be impacted? During my ten-year educational career, I have always known the power of influence that an educator has with his or her students. Since we spend an average of eight to ten hours per day with students in our schools, I am of the opinion that we possess a great opportunity to impress upon students positive ideals and beliefs that will enable them to escape from at-risk status to being an exception to the rules.

As a middle school teacher, I began that opportunity by adopting and implementing a Gentleman's club, scholars club, and FCA (Fellowship of Christian Athletes). I continue to work with these programs, and I also co-chair Mind, Body and Soul, which deals with the academic challenges, soul and psyche of individuals. The wellness and health of young black men is paramount to their success.

As I begin to see males of all ethnicities in school, I realized that a great number of them lack positive male mentors aside from their athletic coaches. I made an intentional effort to get to know my students and at least speak to the parents once per grading period. By doing this, I discovered that the majority of the students did not have both parents in the home. In 2004, I implemented a Gentleman's Club that did community service acts such as canned food drives, Annual Etiquette Dinner, and mentoring at College Station Elementary. Not only did we adopt the name gentleman, we personified it. Each Wednesday of the school year, we vowed to dress in business attire. This not only made us become *noticed* by the students and faculty. More importantly, we emphasized being young men of integrity and character. Members are held to a standard of respect of self and others. There is very little tolerance of the members receiving disciplinary infractions at school. Currently, we ensure that any member struggling academically; will be tutored by a fellow member of the Gentleman's Club. This is a "My Brother's Keeper" concept. During the 2011 Homecoming week festivities, the Gentleman's Club sponsored their first fundraiser to support their own programs.

Our young black men thirst for recognition, and "The Scholars Club" is a way to get more of the young brothers' population recognized for academic excellence and effort. There are four levels of the Scholars Club. The first level consists of the white card holders, who are identified as students with a letter grade improvement from an 'F' to a 'D' or a 'D' to 'C.' The first level tries to reward substantial improvements. The second level is for students who have a 2.5-3.0 GPA. The third level is for the students who have a 3.1-3.75 GPA. The fourth level is for students holding an impressive 3.76-5.0 GPA. The reward system for scholars is that the third and fourth levels get into interscholastic local school events for free, while the first and second levels receive a discount.

The FCA program has actually been around since 1954. Growing up in smaller school districts, administrators and coaches really have had a great opportunity to change communities. My assistant principal Terry 'Bo' Ray introduced me to FCA. I remember vividly the donuts but more importantly, the prayers and lessons that I learned through his teaching of life lessons and Bible application in FCA. During the 2011 school year, our school hosted the first-ever Fields of Faith, which is an FCA student-led worship service with prayer and worship stemming from the King Josiah challenge found in II Chronicles 34. At this event, we had three-hundred-plus students and community members present. Students shared their testimonies. It was awesome. Indeed, students need as much hope as they can possibly receive. Fellowship of Christian Athletes allows coaches and athletes to learn far more than athletic skill, but also spiritual guidance.

Finally, "Mind, Body and Soul" is a four-hour daily summer program. It emphasizes creative expressions through writing and speaking. In addition, we work on problem solving and conflict resolution, as well as identifying our place and purpose as it relates to cultural awareness. The other component is literacy and writing. Initially, the program was only for at-risk black males. We strive to help the entire person through this program by addressing health and wellness, spiritual growth life, and academics. After looking at the data after the first year of the program, I noticed that the young men in attendance were able to improve their behavior at school. I believe that when we build mentor-type relationships with students, they tend to understand that they have had blind spots that keep them from seeing the reality that exists when students' behavior cause them to miss a great deal of school. As a result, the students were enlightened to the importance of the getting an education in a global society. Consequently, we have to give young Black men an opportunity to make intelligent decisions and steer them away from a lifestyle "where ignorance is bliss."

Chapter Ten

Goals are Key to One's Success

Too many of our young men miss this opportunity for positive growth and development due to the absences of a strong father, a great role model, or a safe mentor in their lives.

Dr. Reginald Wilson

State Department of Education Manager
Educational Consultant

It was that time again. Each week we would meet in the boardroom at 7 am. We will be there for about three hours before things got too hot. James Wilson, chair and CEO, will call the meeting to order and set the agenda for the day. James Wilson (my father) is a white collar educational manager for the state department of education and formerly a high school chemistry teacher. Each day he conducts meetings, sends out directives, makes presentations, and lays out a plan of action with explanations why it should work that particular way.

This particular 7 a.m. meeting took place in the family garden. Saturday morning before the mercury rose we were there in the garden standing at full attention. It is there where much of the magic takes place – not just plants growing and producing fruit, but another magic that I did not recognize at the time but now I see quite clearly. As a ninth or tenth grade student, I saw this meeting as nothing more than something that messed up my Saturday morning.

I remember thinking, who does this? None of my friends were up working in a garden. They were able to sleep late and watch cartoons on Saturday mornings.

My brother and I would meet Daddy in the boardroom at 7 a.m. with shovels, picks and the garden hoe. It seemed that every time we met, we were digging up new rocks, pulling up weeds, or making small holes to put some plant or seed in. We would make rows for this or that and patches for something else. Daddy would talk the whole time and ask us questions.

I thought he was just torturing me because he knew I didn't want to be there. Of course, I had the Saturday morning attitude (that I didn't want to be there), but he acted like he didn't notice or didn't care.

I now realize that this time was what we now know as "quality time" with my father, as well as training. From those experiences, I learned how to conduct myself according to "Jim's Law." I received several jewels of wisdom from him that have shaped my character, developed my work ethic and fine-tuned the way I saw things and responded to my environment. Daddy would always use examples and analogies to explain situations and lead you to his conclusion as if they were your own.

On this particular morning, Daddy took the pick and made a straight row from the top of the garden to the bottom. I was instructed to do the same, so I made my row next to his. Daddy had me to stand at the end of the row and compare the two. He asked me if I noticed any differences. I said "no," knowing full well that my row looked like a long snake. He said, "Great!" I then continued and made several additional rows so that we could plant onions or tomatoes or something. After adding five or six more rows of the same kind with my nasty attitude, he stopped me and had me to look again at my rows and his one. He asked me, "How does it look?" I said, "Fine to me." Again, knowing that I had made a mess, but I just wanted to get by. Daddy said, "Reggie I see several things that need to be corrected here. First, your disrespectful attitude about being here in the garden needs to be adjusted. The lie you told about the first row you made, which was wrong, and the continued lie about the remaining rows, which were still wrong. The fact that you would waste time and energy wanting to pass this junk effort off as if it were okay shows me that you don't care about the quality of your work or how it impacts the last name that I have given you. You also made the assumption that I was that slow or stupid (which I am nowhere near) and would let you get by with this fool mess. Son, if I didn't care about you, I would let you get by with this, but because you are mine and a Wilson I cannot allow it."

"Now, you tell me Reggie – what do you think you need to do to fix this?" he asked.

I said, "I need to redo my rows and make them straighter."

Daddy said, "I think that is a good idea," and he added, "This is not about rows in a garden as much as it is about the quality of your work.

This experience and intense discussion helped me to understand the following jewels from Jim's Law.

> **Jim's Jewel #23 – The quality of your work carries your name and identifies who you are.**
>
> **Jim's Jewel #14 – If you establish yourself as a liar, no one will trust you.**
>
> **Jim's Jewel #31 – Wasted time is time loss that will cost you later.**
>
> **Jim's Jewel #43 – Work smarter not harder.**
>
> **Jim's Jewel #53 – Don't be "loud" and "wrong."**

This kind of exchange is critical to the positive development of any young man today. Too many of our young men miss this opportunity for positive growth and development due to the absences of a strong father, a great role model, or a safe mentor in their lives. I think we owe this to each other and to the young men who are not as fortunate as we are.

Chapter Eleven

Responsibility is Not an Emotion – It is a Commitment...

What we must do is step forward now,
and refuse to cede any more ground.

Mr. Jackie Calhoun

High School Administrator

I cannot recall the number of times that I have asked myself: *What are we going to do with these young brothers?* Their chosen paths are so destructive that they are simply going to work themselves right out of extinction. They will not be able to help their families, and will instead be the primary funding source for a generation of entrepreneurs known as prison planners.

When I was asked my thoughts on the crisis facing young black men in public schools, I could only pause and shake my head in disappointment. "So many problems, so few solutions," was my natural response. I thought about my own rearing by my parents, who have children who became doctors, scientists and public school administrators. By any standards, we were poor folks from the country who moved into poverty in the city. Yet we thrived in poverty because black folks in the community cared about their children enough to be a vibrant part of the school experience.

Our parents did not have a lot of education, but public schools during that period of segregation were different. Black parents didn't have to have a tremendous amount of education because our African American teachers were the best and brightest that schools of any race had to offer. Our teachers were a solid combination of male and female, and discipline was almost non-existent. Students respected the staff, and the staff demanded that respect.

I focus on that singular issue because for more than twenty years, I have served primarily as an administrator in charge of discipline in the public schools. Unfortunately, most of the students who have visited me under unpleasant conditions have been black males. I have often gone home in the afternoons after a day of hearing stories of misconduct and mistreatment from two separate sources. While teachers say that black boys engage in disruptive and sometimes reprehensible behavior, the attitude of the black male student is almost always mild and even docile in my presence. It's hard to fathom that these students represent what is written on a disciplinary referral. Yet at the same time, several of the students' behaviors represent just what is written on the referral.

A majority of young black men have become walking profanity machines. With an alarming frequency, they engage in inappropriate, explicit and profane use of language in anybody's presence. They have no sense of decency, as it is associated with dress or conduct. In short, a vast majority of young African American males have followed the most negative stereotypes imaginable, and engaged and committed themselves on a continuous path to nowhere. They lack social skills and refuse to acknowledge that they are at fault.

When I engage in disciplinary conferences with young black males, I often ask them about why they think the behavior is acceptable. The response more often than not is, "My mother lets me do this, so who are they to tell me I can not?" I am forced to consider that a child's parent doesn't have enough respect for self to empower this kid to make this type of response. I then have a reflective moment and think back. What would my parents do to me if I gave that type of response to the principal who had caught me, or had received a report of wrongdoing concerning me?

You notice I said parent(s) and that is a large part of the problem. My parent(s) would have come to school and literally beat the hell out of me. If not, they would have met the principal after school, because he would have come by the house after work. You see, we all lived in the same neighborhoods. This too is a large part of our community problem. A negative response to a teacher or administrator was not tolerated during my time in the Black Public Schools, or immediately after integration. The respect factor was simply too great. Black kids and especially black boys knew better. Cursing at school or fighting at school was tantamount to signing a death wish at home. The extension cord would serve notice that intolerant behavior was not acceptable.

When I said parents in an early sentence, I meant parents. I meant extended family. I meant the whole community. I meant aunts and uncles, and neighbors who looked out for kids and whipped them as though they were their own. It was the rule of the neighborhood that Ms. Jones' kids were my mother's kids as well when she saw them doing something wrong. I often reflect back on that time and ask the two million dollar question: Where did it go? Where did the respect factor and the culture of high achievement disappear? When did low achievement and lower expectations invade and take over the culture of young black males? When did rap stars and professional athletes become more important that teachers, and even parents? When did a concert or club become more important than family outings and Sunday morning church? The correct response should be never, but sadly that's not the case.

But I do know who is to blame. If you're a parent of a young black male and you've never been to a parent conference, look in the mirror. If you're a father who can't name any of your son's teachers from the first through the fourth grade, just look in the mirror. Chances are, they only had one teacher per grade, and you missed the mark on that one.

What we must do is step forward now and refuse to cede any more ground. If that means having a heart-to-heart talk with the Good Lord first, then get it done now and move toward your son. It might take some tough love and a reappearing act, but whatever the cost, it must be done. An absent black father cannot be a duplicitous process that your son engages in when he forms his own family. It is never too late to start the process of healing from within.

I cannot tell you how few black men I have had in for parent conferences with black boys over the years. If I want to call someone's father, the typical response is, "do not know my daddy's number," or "He does not live with us," or "He is not going to come." I think, garbage, and I call anyway. Unfortunately, most of the children are correct. They know what an absent dad will not be doing on their behalf: intervening.

Seven out of every ten suspensions I handle involves black boys. This simply can not be the end-all. When black boys, or any child, miss school and experience long-term absenteeism, they suffer in ways that often cannot be repaired. They lose valuable instruction that will have a disproportionate effect on them. Often black males are two to three grades behind in basic skills and lack the ability to catch up in a timely fashion. This sad scenario is often compounded by a lack of assistance from the parents in the home, who don't have the basic skills to assist.

At the end of the day, everyone else has had their chance to make a significant difference, or a minor difference, in the lives of young black boys – and now it's our turn. It's not something we can run away from; it's not something we can hide beneath the shelf or in the closet. What black boys do in the immediate future in terms of academic and social successes or lack thereof will directly impact the communities in which we live and in where we hope to raise our families. The uplifting of a people is contingent upon the actions of a few of us talking the time to start a new movement of responsible black men seeking to change the nature, conditions, and hope for young black boys. All we need is one man at a time, lending his very best to one at-risk black boy at a time. It's a simple solution that requires more giving than receiving. According to II Corinthians 8:1: *Christian giving is God's activity of Grace.* Giving is not a work; we are just trustees and stewards of God's possessions. It's time to give some back. It's time to go to work.

Chapter Twelve

Faith

Boys need big brothers, fathers, uncles, cousins, ministers, neighbors, teachers and every man in the community to encourage healthy decisions.

Floyd Williams

"This is blood money," said Reverend Lester, my mentor, who would regularly check on me. My freshman year in college was my first taste of freedom, and I had lost my mind by overindulging, socializing and making the wrong choices. Initially, I had a track scholarship and an academic scholarship through my father's work at the shipyards, but my overdoing it in the fun department caused me to become ineligible for sports and lose the scholarship.

Reverend Lester was a chemist and associate minister of the Community Baptist Church of Greater Milwaukee, the church that raised me. Throughout high school, Reverend Lester and his wife had me over to their house for dinner, gave me savings bonds and tutored me when I needed help.

Now, he stood before me telling me what time it was and how I needed to man up. Reverend Lester said the opportunities I had did not come easy.

My parents worked long hours to provide so that I could have all that I was enjoying right then. I needed to understand that it was not just me, Floyd E. Williams, Jr., attending Marquette University, but rather I was the embodiment of the work, sweat and sacrifice of my mother, father and all the people who brought me up from childhood to young adulthood. I was the first person in my family to attend college. The opportunity to stand on collegiate grounds and decide my destiny and create a path of my own doing was afforded to me because of the work of my elders. I needed to recognize and represent.

I was indebted to Reverend Lester for giving me the real talk before I permanently closed too many doors for myself. At the time, I was on academic probation, and it was the second semester. One of my sharpest skills has always been observation. I looked around at the students who were achieving and mimicked their study habits – attending class, taking notes, conferring with students and preparing for upcoming tests. It worked and by the end of the semester, I had proved myself a scholar and was back making the grades.

I came from a traditional nuclear family with two working parents. My mother cleaned luxury apartments on the affluent east side of Milwaukee, and my father unloaded ships at the docks at the Port of Milwaukee and was part-owner of a tavern.

Both had made it through the tenth grade in school before they had to graduate to adult life and work so as to contribute to the family. My parents were from Texas and were part of the great migration north in the 1960s. Millions of African Americans came north in search of a better life. My father's siblings moved also, but my mother's family remained in Houston, Texas.

I was the youngest of three children. My brother, Larry, was thirteen years old and sister, Gladys, ten years old when I appeared on the scene. Being that much younger than my siblings, my mother and father would frequently take me to work with them. They were testimony to a strong work ethic. Even as a small boy, I was given tasks to accomplish, such as sweeping floors and emptying trash cans. I would carefully observe the dynamics of the interactions between adults, listen to their jokes and see how people negotiated jobs, pay and other adult issues. It was a rich pre-school experience that I remember well.

We lived northwest of downtown and when I reached school age, I attended the local elementary school, Hopkins Street School. In elementary school, I earned good grades. Because I scored high on the standardized tests, the guidance counselor told my parents I should apply to the gifted and talented middle school.

My neighborhood was a place where people raised families, barbecued on Saturdays and took pride in their homes and yards, but there was always the unknown lurking around the corner. Athletic shoes tied together by the laces hung from telephone lines marking places where kids had been jumped. Those kids lost their music players, cash and pride. My elementary school playground was not safe. Every basketball court was a testing ground to demonstrate skill, grit and strategy. Any friendly game could turn into a fight if the opponent's ego was hurt. To show disapproval, the opponent would put an elbow in someone's ribs. After a few of those, one had to fight or walk away and be tagged as a coward.

One time, I was playing a one-on-one basketball game with a boy named Royree, in my back alley. The score turned in my favor, and he was not happy. Royree elbowed me in my face as I went for a lay-up. Then, it happened again, and I just knew I was going to have to fight him. Suddenly, my mom stepped out of the house and asked what was going on. Royree swore at her and told her to mind her own business. At the time, my brother Larry, thirteen years older and fresh out of the military, was upstairs resting. He heard Royree's words and promptly came outside with a gun tucked into his belt.

Royree said, "Oh, so you got people? I got people, too." Then, he left, but it was not over.

My brother parked himself on the hood of his car in front of the house, waiting. When my dad came home from work, he readied his shotgun. Later on, Royree and twenty gang members came walking down the middle of the street. My dad came out of the house with his gun. My mom, worried about what might happen, pleaded with him to come into the house.

Royree and his gang stopped about twenty feet in front of Larry. The leader was Royree's cousin, Chris, who went to high school with Larry. Chris stepped out to talk with Larry, and they exchanged some words in private. Then, Chris announced, "From this day on, leave him and everyone in this house alone." After that, there was no trouble. I could ride the bus or walk down the street, and I was not bothered.

Throughout middle school, high school and college, I was shown the ropes by my cousin, Claude. Eight years older than me, Claude took me to high school football and basketball games and track meets. Once in high school, I attended events sponsored by Phi Beta Sigma Fraternity, Inc., and previewed collegiate activities. I was introduced to young black men and women who were in leadership roles. Claude became an engineer and respected leader in his community. The time spent tagging along helped me see which way I wanted to go and how to get there.

In college, there were many leadership opportunities. Initially, I was on an engineering track. I participated in a mentoring program that provided monthly trainings and after an internship at an international company where I was assigned the project of redesigning the shop floor to eliminate laborers, I became disinterested in engineering. I wanted a job that helped people, not one that helped people out of their jobs. My good friend's mentor, Mr. Wild, invited me to come to Chicago with him for a weekend to hang out and go places. I did not have any money, nor did my friend, but we were invited as his guests so the price was right. All weekend, Mr. Wild and his friends talked about the education field. It sounded like the opportunity I wanted – a chance to serve my community and work with young people.

When I returned from that weekend, I signed up to work with the Youth Leadership Academy, an organization that exclusively provided tutoring for African American boys. On Saturdays, I led students through tutorials. I also led a six-week summer program. At Marquette University there was Upward Bound, a high school mentoring program. I became an Upward Bound counselor and facilitated pre-college programs and experiences for high school students. My path was decided. All of these experiences confirmed that my undergraduate degree should be in education. I completed my degree and became a middle school science teacher. It was fulfilling and satisfying, and I knew I had made the right choice. Leadership opportunities began to present themselves and after acquiring an administration license, I became a principal. While I was one of the youngest principals in the district, I kept looking forward and seeking more knowledge, and earned a doctorate in leadership for the advancement of learning and service.

I always remembered Reverend Lester's words that I did not arrive where I am on my own. President Barack Obama once imparted this same message, reminding us that we are helped along by someone.

Throughout my life, I have been the recipient of understanding, encouragement, protection, shelter, mentoring, tutoring, counseling, kindness and generosity. My success is not mine alone. It belongs to my family, church and community.

Boys need big brothers, fathers, uncles, cousins, ministers, neighbors, teachers and every man in the community to encourage healthy decisions. Our responsibility to youth is to help out wherever we can and give back what we received. Our lives are not our own; they were paid for with the blood of our ancestors. It is our responsibility to be mentors, tutors and guardians to our boys so they can continue the cycle of giving back to the black community and the world.

Chapter Thirteen

The Will to Succeed

"Go to college," my mom would say. And I would respond with, "How do I do that?"

Jeremy S. Owoh

High School Principal

Who taught me what it means to be a real man? What or whom prepared me to be a husband? What or who prepared me to be a true father? Who were my examples of what a young African American male in today's society is supposed to emulate? These questions went unanswered until I became a husband and a father and, like many of us, I had to construct the answers on my own.

My story, like many others who look and sound like me, is constructed like a never-ending labyrinth. Most of my life I found myself wandering here and there without a clear path or a clear ending point. I was born to Eula and Sunny Owoh. My mother was born and raised in the southeast quadrant of Arkansas and my dad was born in Enugu State, Nigeria. This was a unique but destined union. However, my parents' union did not last long – six years. It was long enough to produce three boys who were added to the millions of other black boys in today's society: STATISTICS. These three boys could have ended up like the vast majority of black boys in today's society.

Not long after my parents' divorce, my mother met a man who would become my stepfather. Jessie would become the father that I never had. My stepfather was a role model when it came to working hard and taking care of your family; however, my stepfather never attended a college. You see; it did not matter that he did not go to college because he worked hard every day to provide for his children and three little boys who did not have his biological makeup.

Reflecting over the past thirty-two years, I have never heard him complain about it, not one time. Actually, he tends to brag about his "sons" to anyone who will listen. He is a true role model of a man who takes care of his responsibility – and another man's responsibility.

Growing up in rural Arkansas produced advantages and disadvantages for these three little black boys. Expectations for our community were low, but the expectations for my household were very high. However, these expectations were not always clear. My mother always said, "Do your best so that you can do something with your life." She made us go to the local library to check out books and we would read all summer and on the weekends. We could not attend parties or hang out at the local hangout spots. My mom was very particular about our extracurricular activities. "Go to college," my mom would say. And I would respond with, "How do I do that?" Still no role model to emulate...

I always achieved relatively high grades in school. I excelled in the band and other extracurricular activities – but for what goal? I knew that I did not want to stay in Camden, but I did not know anything about how to get to college or just how to get out of Camden. Eventually, my twin brother and I applied for college our spring semester in high school; we also enlisted in the Army Reserve.

Toward the end of high school spring semester, I was admitted into the University of Central Arkansas. In June, my twin brother and I left for basic training, but I quickly realized the military was not for me. The drill sergeants knew it, my family knew it and I knew it. Still searching for a role model...

My collegiate years were very eventful with parties, academia, fraternity life and a full-time job. To be honest, I did not think about life after college until my fifth year of college. I had a full-time job and I was a full-time student.

I started my collegiate year as a marketing major but quickly realized that it was not for me. Since I was attending the university on a band scholarship, I thought about majoring in music; however, when I lost my scholarship that thought quickly came and departed. I wandered around corner after corner in life searching for my calling. What am I supposed to do with my life? What am I going to do after I finish school?

I thought and reflected on my life...what did I enjoy

doing? I realized that I grew up with a love for reading, and I loved working with people. I decided to become an English Education major. Unbeknownst to me, this decision would send my life spiraling – not downward but upward. It was a struggle to matriculate through the degree program, especially being the only black male in most of my classes. It was a struggle because I did not have anyone to confide in about my academic struggles nor my self-worth deficiencies. I quickly realized that I was on an island surrounded by natives, and I was not a native of this land. I was in uncharted territory. Where was a role model with whom I could identify? After several struggles and jolts to my confidence in being an English teacher, I matriculated through the program one class after another.

I could have probably done that for a while, but my mom asked me one day, "When do you plan on graduating?" One year later, my twin brother, his wife and I graduated from the university. And with that, I started my adult life as a black male educator.

"Take the first step in faith. You don't have to see the whole staircase, just take the first step."
- *Martin Luther King*

The years in the trenches as an educator in an urban setting have taught me that I alone have great influence on my students. I can recall a time that a parent called me and said,

"Mr. Owoh, Chris is always saying, 'But Mr. Owoh said this and that'. He listens to everything that you say and pays close attention to everything you do." At that moment, I realized that my calling was to be a teacher. Even with strong fathers at home, it is important strong black role models always surround our black boys.

Why is it imperative that this happens? With all of the negative attention that black youth receive on the news and in other media outlets, it is essential that black youth receive the positive support and the reoccurring assurance that they are making positive strides. If all our black boys see are negative images in popular culture, then we have done them an injustice.

It is my prayer and hope that black males realize the power that they have with our youth. My wife once told me, "J, when you walk in the room, people take notice." I asked her what she meant by that statement. She merely stated, "J, people take notice of black men who speak well and carry themselves with confidence". I am still confused with where this act of confidence came from. I realized that even though I haven't been looking up to one person, I had created the man that I wanted to be. It was my secret that I lacked the confidence that people saw in me. But I began to realize the importance of setting high standards for oneself because you never know when people are watching you. It's also important that we take the time to stop and converse with our youth.

"I believe that unarmed truth and unconditional love

will have the final word in reality. This is why right, temporarily defeated, is stronger than evil triumphant."
- *Martin Luther King*

If a child can idolize a basketball player whom he has never known, then he can respect and look up to a man who is always supporting and listening to him. So many of our youth are always talked to and never listened to when they need help.

President Obama stated, "We are the ones that we have been waiting for." This has so many meanings for me. In my state of mind today, it answers the question that I have always had: *Who will be my role model?* The answer comes throughout these pages. It is men, like me, who decide to look back, stoop down and not only pull a brother up with him but to also teach the younger brothers how to stand toe-to-toe with their counterparts.

Credentials by themselves do not mean anything, but group the credentials with resilience, perseverance and self-worth and you will then be a powerhouse – an African American male with substance. Why should black men mentor black youth? The answer is simple: it is our calling.

If we do not mentor our youth, who will? We should not allow one African American youth to come within our presence without taking the time and having a conversation with him. We need to ask our youth about their plans and future goals. How will they obtain their goals? We should point them to the right resources that will aid them in achieving their goals. I have seen so many successful black males who turn their backs on each other out of fear that the other will take what they have. Why do we do this?

Interacting with younger fraternity brothers has taught me that not only is it my duty to give back to them (to devote dedicated time to listen to them and give quality feedback), it is IMPERATIVE that I do. If young men are not given direction, we allow them to wander about blindly and hopelessly.

"Whatever affects one directly, affects all indirectly. I can never be what I ought to be until you are what you ought to be. This is the interrelated structure of reality."
- *Martin Luther King*

As an administrator, I make it my priority to stop and talk with all my students, but especially my male students. Male students are a special breed of individuals, almost delicate. Males are delicate because the wrong interactions, experience or response can send them spiraling in the opposite direction that you want them to go. It is important for us to remember never to demean any of our students but especially our male students because for some of them, their reputation or image is all that they have. This is true for almost all males, but especially black males.

While my profession may cause me some headache and

frustration here and there, it's all worth it when a former student comes and says, "Mr. O, thanks for all that you have done for me…for listening to me and never giving up on me." It only takes one to two conversations to redirect a male who is having difficulty with making the right decisions.

"Train up a child in the way he should go; even when he is old he will not depart from it."
- *Martin Luther King*

Chapter Fourteen

The Crisis is Real

I believe there is something we can do to reclaim our males, and it starts with re-shifting the male into his proper position in the household.

Marquis Cooper, Sr. M. Ed (ABD)

High School Counselor
Author

When posed the question of "Why black men must save black boys in America's public schools," I began to examine the many challenges that our black males are faced with each and every day. I was born and raised in a small town in Eastern Arkansas called Marianna, Arkansas. I grew up in a blended family, which means a family that is formed when separate families are united by marriage. My mother bore twelve children during her first marriage, and my father had nine children during his first marriage. The story goes, when my siblings found out that my mother was pregnant with me, they all told her that the only thing she needed to bring home was a cat. Needless to say, I became the twenty-second child, which completed my family. I'm the only child they had together, so for the most part I considered myself to be an only child because I grew up without the rest of the "football" team.

My son: observe the commandments of your father, and do not forsake the teaching of your mother. Proverbs 6:20

While growing up, I heard stories of many credible individuals from Marianna such as Charlie Flowers, Oliver Lake, Robert McFerrin, Oscar Polk, Jean Yarbrough, James Banks, Anna Strong, Roy Lewellen, C. Calvin Smith, and Rodney Slater, who served as the United States Secretary of Transportation from 1997 to 2001. Marianna at one point and time was a city to be proud of, but during the late 1980s, the image of the town slowly began to fall apart. The story of the Chambers brothers, (leaders of a Marianna to Detroit crack cocaine connection), created a dark shadow that the city has never been able to live down. Some people believed that if you were from Marianna, then your fate rested in being a thug, murderer, and a criminal or drug dealer. Recently, Marianna once again became the focus of negative media attention following the stories of Curtis Vance (convicted of killing KATV anchorwoman Ann Presley), Maurice Clemmons (killed by police who sought him for the shooting deaths of four police officers in Washington State), and now Operation Delta blues (a major drug raid that netted 70 indictments). The efforts of many positive individuals have now been overshadowed by the latest stories of individuals that had ties with Marianna.

Past stories and events like the ones mentioned led us to create the "Our Story" Youth Leadership Conference in Marianna. One of the missions of "Our Story" is to give our black males a sense of pride, responsibility, and hope to achieve success despite the negative circumstances that surround them.

In 2009, the U.S. Census Bureau conducted a study on the number of single parents and the amount of child support they receive (does not represent all single parents). The bureau reported that there was an estimated 13.7 million single parents who had custody of 21.8 million children age 21 and under. Mothers accounted for 82.6 percent and fathers accounted for 17.4 percent. Yes, that is true. The results prove that we have more single women raising children alone. The numbers don't lie. There are very few positive male role models in homes.

At some point in history, we created this seed of irresponsibility in our males. As a result, the prison system is overpopulated and we have done nothing to change the outcome. I believe there is something we can do to reclaim our males, and it starts with re-shifting the male into his proper position in the household.

Please allow me to paint a picture and make it clear. The standard order for a "two" parent household is that of the father, wife, son and daughter. But a plan was devised many years ago that changed the structure of the family, especially the positioning of the male. In many African American homes across this country, the family structure looks like the following: You have the son (in an unknown spot), mother (in the father's spot), daughter (behind her mother out of her spot), and the father (totally removed from the family, he has no spot). Here is an illustration for those of you who are visual learners; please read from left to right.

Normal Family Structure	Father (head of household)	Wife (beside the head)	Son (beside the mother)	Daughter (beside the brother)
Son (positioned beside his mom on the left side)	Wife (positioned where the father was)	Daugher (positioned behind her mom)	Father (positioned nowhere)	**Dysfunctional Family Structure**

The dysfunctional family structure has caused even the formation of the chart to become dysfunctional. When this style of familial transfer takes charge, it has a profound effect on the entire family unit, but more so with the male. The African American male population has been far more affected than any other ethnic group. The African American population is only 13.5 percent of the American population. The crucial problem that has now arisen is how to change a family structure that has been perfected in the life of the African American male for the past 300 years.

The crisis for the black male occupying an unknown spot has created a major crisis within the black community. This crisis can be seen in most homes, neighborhoods, schools, college campuses, and even on jobs. What is the crisis you might ask? The crisis as it relates to the men in America looks like this:

*A nation of pants **sagging,** interchangeable grill mouth* *wearing,* bling bling *wanting,* big rims *seeking, foul language* *using,* sports driven *dreamers, fashion statement* *makers, non* vision *having,* no purpose in life *wanting,* silly acting *daily,* non identity *having,* name *seekers*

The above scenario exists because, "The man is out of place, the woman is displaced, and the children have become misplaced." (Marquis Cooper). The good news is there's still hope to change the fate of many black males in public schools. We can no longer allow 72 percent of our black males to fail in public schools because their fathers chose not to be in their lives. We can no longer allow the aforementioned crisis to continue to be the "norm" for black males. We can no longer make excuses for not reaching back to save our young black males.

The plight of the African American male in society, as well as those in public schools, seems to be getting worse by the minute. A lot of young men have no lamp (father) to observe, so often they are being guided by the light; (mother) only. A light (mother) without a lamp (father) is dangerous. A lot of young black males have no idea of what it takes to be a good leader because they've never seen one. Tupac echoes this message in his song "Keep Ya Head Up" from his *Still I Rise* album. He states, "Say there ain't no hope for the youth and the truth is it ain't no hope for the future." I have to agree wholeheartedly with Tupac because if we believe there is no hope for the youth then we are doomed. There is hope to save this generation of young black males, but it all starts with knowing, believing, and internalizing the power of *it's ok.*

The circle of change for our black males in public schools begins with knowing the power of *it's ok.* So my fellow males, *it's ok* to be intelligent. *It's ok* to break and lead at the same time. *It's ok* not to use slang every time you speak. *It's ok* to speak correct English. *It's ok* if you do not want to play sports. *It's ok* to keep your pants up and not sag. *It's ok* if you don't want rims on your car. *It's ok* if you don't want to act silly while in class. *It's ok* for you to open the door anytime a lady is present. *It's ok* to be respectful at all times. *It's ok* to shake a young lady's hand and say goodnight. *It's ok* to use your manners. *It's ok* to clean your room. *It's ok* to vacuum the house. *It's ok* to be a leader. *It's ok* not to use profanity. *It's ok* to have a vision in life. *It's ok* to know your purpose in life. Most importantly, *it's ok* to be you.

Through the power of *it's ok,* back men can save black boys in America's public schools. Frederick Douglass states, "It is far easier to build strong children than to repair broken men." I believe what Frederick Douglass stated years ago. The question is, do you?

Chapter Fifteen

Beyond the Surface

*I believe that education begins as a civil right,
a freedom-birthed opportunity to develop
our minds, to condition our perception of reality,
and to help shape our character.*

Dr. John W. Gilliame

High School Teacher

My name is Dr. John W. Gilliame, the proud son of Mr. and Mrs. John W. Gilliame, Sr. I grew up with two older siblings in a small, poor rural community in North Little Rock called *Dixie Addition.* My father left home when I was four years old, leaving my mother to fend and provide for three children with limited resources and minimal education. Though growing up in Dixie wasn't difficult, there were challenges and obstacles that I had to overcome and confront. I was just an average black kid learning how to adapt, adjust and cope with the normal problems that other kids in the area had to face: how to stay out of trouble, away from alcohol and drugs, how to defend yourself, and how to find a way to make some money *legally.*

Schools were fully integrated by the time I enrolled and my educational journey began in a place called North Heights Elementary School. It was a very comfortable place for me, and when I was in the third grade, it was brought to my mother's attention that I had extraordinary intellectual abilities.

I now understand that this gift was an anointing given by God with a specific purpose for my future. Nevertheless, it brought me unmerited favor through grammar school, middle school, and throughout my high school term. Being fairly gifted in athletics, I was blessed to spend a lot of quality time around my white friends, their families and acquaintances. They were very kind to me; they encouraged me and shared resources and ideas with me.

From those encounters, I knew then that I wanted something more out of life than what was being provided for me at that present time. I was determined to beat the odds of social-economic stereotypes and the biological genetic predictions of family, friends and neighbors. I witnessed several individuals waste their lives away; some ended up in prison, and some died prematurely.

My newfound relationship with the Lord in my late teens truly placed me on the right path of success, helping me to be committed, disciplined, and faithful in my educational goals as well as my spiritual life. I have to admit that growing up with no father figure in the home, receiving government-provided subsidies, and not being conditioned to be responsible caused me to struggle in the adjustment from the teenage years into young adulthood. Yes, I was doing great in college; I enjoyed the classroom atmosphere, but upon graduation I found myself with the need to find a job. What I discovered through experience is that your perception of the world and your life is your reality, and that you cannot live beyond what you know or what you have not been exposed to. *I realized that I had to develop a different mindset, learn how to be disciplined and professional, and hold myself accountable.* I sought after mentors and seasoned counselors to educate me on social etiquette. *I learned that clothes don't make the man, but they introduce the man* – and that people see *what* you are before they know *who* you are. The Bible teaches that safety exists in the multitude of counseling, and I realized that learning from a mentor instead of experience is a better way to learn. A mentor helps you to avoid issues of pain, setbacks and disappointment.

My greatest assets and qualities, as an educator, stem from the nurturing patterns of past instructors. Most students and especially my African-American boys bond and conform to my instructional philosophy because they sense that I really care and that I can fully relate to their emotional and social struggles. I believe that in the initial stages of a class that the teacher should try to make a divine connection with each student, attempt to establish a positive report, and create a common denominator to form the instructional relationship.

With African-American boys the relationship must be established before the learning can take place; students need a pledge of confidence and trust from the teacher before they yield themselves to new ideas, correction and discipline. In other words, they must know you care before they know what you say.

The more you give in terms of time, extracurricular activity support or perhaps even a dollar here and there to help out on lunch, the more they will take in terms of instructional content, advice and a good *chewing out* if needed. Students can't learn if they resent the teacher, nor can they learn if they fear or distrust the teacher. Sometimes as teachers, as well as most adults, we have a tendency to forget that we were once teenagers experiencing the same challenges that our children are facing today. And to be quite honest, our children's problems and obstacles are far more amplified and magnified due to changes in social norms, family values and technology. Our current status quo as a nation describes our children as weaker but wiser due to the exposure of negative immoral literature, music, and technological entertainment.

As teachers, many of us have an "eight-track" mentality in a classroom full of "iPod thinking" students whose bodies and minds are undergoing dramatic changes, with possibly 90 to 95 percent of their thoughts being sexually related and linked to some form of deviant activity. Again the Bible indicates that foolishness is bound in the heart of a child, and that the rod of correction would drive it far from them. For certain, teachers should be that *rod of correction* through communication and modeling, attempting to illustrate what behavior and attitude is acceptable. Several students are left to fend for themselves via default as well as by omission and commission; many are victims of parental neglect, sexual abuse, and parental absentee due to work.

I believe that education begins as a civil right, a freedom-birthed opportunity to develop our minds, to condition our perception of reality, and to help shape our character. It demands responsibility and integrity from those who reach certain plateaus and levels within its ranks. According to Dr. Martin Luther King, education is deemed as the social liaison that bridges the gaps between Blacks and Whites. It's been stated once that a beautiful mind is far more beneficial and lucrative than dazzling curves and in the long run, could mean the difference between poverty and wealth, and happiness and discontentment. The consequences for the absence of education and knowledge could be very regrettable and devastating to one's socioeconomic credibility, health, and eventually their lifespan. Education is an application used to help every student to reach that level of success according to what they perceive success to be. I believe that a good teacher is one that constantly and consistently draws forth the best effort and potential that each student has to give. It's very important for teachers to raise the confidence and self-esteem of each student according to their individual abilities, not comparing them to others. As educational and society leaders, teachers are leaders, and they do leave lasting impressions whether they be positive or negative.

As an educated black man, I don't think it would seem strange if I was rather biased in favor of black males' progress in education and in the classroom. Research indicates that most young black males struggle in making the transition from grammar school into middle school. The experience they gain at the middle school level will either catapult them forward toward graduating from high school, or send them on a downward spiral of gangs, drugs, alcohol, and imminent high school dropout. Speaking from experience, it can really be difficult with hormonal changes, rebellious attitudes, not having nice things that you see other kids have, and last but not least, not having a father-figure in the home to guide or model what you need to see or avoid. I believe that Black males set the standards in educational research with regards to benchmarks and improvements in literacy and math. I truly believe it is safe to say that you can rest assured that when black males are learning, everybody is learning. They are the thermostats that set the tone for establishing objectives for targeted areas of improvement. Being in the mass majority of seemingly every negative aspect of society, they represent the "true grit" struggle in the trenches of improvement across the board. My soul will not rest until every black male in a public school reads at grade level, writes using standard English, and has the skill level to not only attend, but succeed, in a college learning environment.

My commitment is to make sure that all of our young African American brothers have every opportunity in life to reach their potential. It's the least I can do, for all of those who did before me.

Chapter Sixteen

Up Where We Belong

Now more than ever there is a need for men to

*galvanize our efforts to stand up and be counted
in the lives of children. A clarion call has gone out
to help students and in particular, black boys.
Up where we belong, "Granite Mountains."*

Don Booth

Principal
State Department Consultant

I grew up as a teenager in the South during the late 1960s and early 1970s when the nation was at the height of a social and political mandate from the government. In 1964, they passed a bill to give those – Blacks – who did not have much just a little more, but it only went so far. The reform movement not only was a necessary action on the part of government, but it also was needed to assist a group of people – Blacks – who had been disenfranchised with the promise of the American

Dream. Unfortunately, this movement was not congruent with the philosophy of the political machine, nor was it on the agenda of the white privileged faction that regulated and controlled the aforementioned machine. A race that endured two hundred years of adverse social and political behavior was now postured to go forth and do great things for a country that once incarcerated them.

I lived in the most scenic and picturesque community in the city of Little Rock, Arkansas. The community sat atop of the city at an elevation of nearly nine hundred feet above ground level. Over the years, politicians and city managers have tried and tried to gain possession of this land to build expensive condominiums and high-rise apartments. The selling point of this community can be observed from dusk to dawn. You can literally stand anywhere in the community and see the movement of the entire city.

The only reason that the "powers that be" did not continue efforts to acquire the land was because it was located "across the tracks" in a less desirable area of the city. And I knew the feeling of disenfranchisement and hopelessness all too well due to the fact that I lived in this community, known as the largest public housing project in the state of Arkansas.

It was named Booker Homes and affectionately called Granite Mountain. Granite Mountain was a place that was relentless in its pursuit to teach its residents the value of perseverance and resiliency. This housing project, for all intents and purposes, was supposedly the first stop for hundreds of people before moving on to a bigger and better existence. As months turned into years, my parents and hundreds of other families came to the realization that they would be non-participants in the American Dream. In time, the quest for a better life became a distant memory, and they surrendered to the fact that leaving the community was not an option open to them, so they settled in and made the best of their impending future.

Granite Mountain was no different than any other ghetto established by the government to colonize the black race. It had your garden variety of pimps, drug dealers, dropouts, winos, prostitutes, welfare mothers and, of course, many decent, law-abiding citizens. My community was the conversation piece of the city and was highlighted on the evening news on a daily basis. We made the news so often that it created the erroneous perception that Granite Mountain was not a community but rather a city within a city. What was evident throughout the community was the presence of black males as head of households.

Most, if not all, were hard-working men who believed in providing for and protecting their families. Most fathers had to carpool to work due to economic conditions and the fact that very few families owned an automobile. Although fathers were a huge presence in most homes, many did not possess the same urgency for being faithful members of the church as did the women. They were rarely seen in any church on Sundays, but the mothers, wives or significant others and the children flooded the various churches. It was not uncommon to have five or six churches in any given Black community, and I dare not discuss the issue of the white-owned liquor and grocery stores also prevalent within these communities. The role of church leaders, pastors specifically, was most important in the lives of the residents of this Black community. The Sunday sermon brought hope to those who dared to dream of a better day and brighter future for their race and children.

My mother was an ordained missionary and our home church was started in the home of my grandparents. The cornerstone of the family church revealed my lineage. Religion played a crucial role in the lives of families living in the housing project because it was essential to believe in something bigger than them.

The belief in a higher power was more than just a religion; it provided a spiritual outlet for maintaining hope, a belief that God would deliver them from the bondage and oppression placed upon them by society's majority. I must state that the mothers were stalwarts in the family. Their words were law and beyond contestation. Every morning, many of the mothers donned white uniforms, the official attire for domestic workers who usually performed household duties for white families, as they stood at the bus stop.

It was so impressive to see them hold their heads high after working for clients who probably patterned themselves after the characters depicted in the *New York Times* bestselling novel, *The Help.* Nevertheless, the one common denominator each parent in the community understood was the importance of education.

Education in a predominantly black school was like none other. Teachers typically displayed a vested interest in each student and elucidated the theme of being able to compete against the white students. I can remember there being only three male teachers on the elementary school faculty, but the one who made education interesting was my sixth grade teacher, Marvin O. Woods. Many days were spent heavily engaged in developing an understanding of English and math skills because he felt that possessing an acute grasp of the English language and having a strong background in computing numbers could possibly be the trump card that would afford us the opportunity to compete at the top of the food chain.

At the time, I was totally obtuse and did not understand the significance of the hard work we put into studying. I owe a great deal of gratitude to Mr. Woods for his insistence that we believe in being the best. Little did I know that I would encounter another man in junior high who would take a vested interest in me since, as he stated, "I had a chip on my shoulder." Mr. James Mathis was his name, and he held the position of assistant principal.

Mr. Mathis took me out of the traditional or "regular" classes and placed me in honor classes. I rebelled every day because most of my friends were in traditional classes and that was where I wanted to be.

However, Mr. Mathis thought differently. For the next three years, he challenged me to compete and excel until I internalized and understood the meaning of intrinsic value. I matriculated in college and earned a bachelor of arts degree in elementary and special education. I taught in public schools for six years, three at the elementary level and three at the junior high level. Later, I resigned my teaching position to work for the state's Department of Education.

Two years into my tenure with the Department of Education, I received a phone call from an elementary school principal asking if I would consider accepting a position as her assistant principal. I did not even know this principal and was pleased with the offer, but I had to ask, "Why me?" She said she had received favorable references for me and due to my familiarity with the Granite Mountain community, which was the primary area where most of her students lived, my assistance could prove quite beneficial to the students. My response was a resounding "Yes". I believed this was an opportunity to return to my calling and possibly impact the lives of students, as well as give back that which was truly and surely given to me – to champion the cause for all children. I was returning to the very place I had left my heart two years prior.

I remember one year during Christmas break I received a phone call from a parent who desperately asked if I would speak with his daughter Crystal, a sixth grader, regarding her very disrespectful behavior toward him and his wife. Of course I did not mind, but I had to ask why he felt compelled to ask me. He replied that I was the "only adult his daughter believed in and trusted."

What I failed to disclose is that this parent combed the telephone book and called every person with my last name until he was able to reach me. My mind vacillated on that conversation for an extended period of time – a white man called upon me to assist in bringing a change to his household. It was then that I realized the old saying is true, "A person who is hungry really doesn't care who feeds him and he who is naked doesn't care who clothes him." The tipping point for bringing people together is caring.

Twelve years later, a former student who is now a teacher came to my school to get my signature for permission to use my name in a book of poems she had written and was having published. The poem was titled, *The Smell of Security.* It talked about how my cologne permeated the hallways, and how that very smell made her feel secure and know that nothing bad would befall her under my watch. She also told me that while attending Vanderbilt University she had aspirations of becoming a doctor. She went on to explain that I was her motivation for changing her major from biology to education.

She said it was my interaction with her and the other students during her elementary years that made her choose the path of the teaching profession. She wanted to be a part of a profession that moves and motivates students to reach for their dreams. These are just two of the many examples that I have been fortunate enough to experience in my thirty years of educating.

I also can remember times when I questioned my decision to teach, but not one time have I questioned my desire or motivation to teach. I have met many students on my educational path of thirty-three years and not all were the type of students that teachers desire to have in their classrooms. Still, I am compelled to do all I can to help them along the way and demonstrate a concerted effort to make a difference in their lives.

Now more than ever there is a need for men to galvanize our efforts to stand up and be counted in the lives of children. A clarion call has gone out to help students and in particular, black boys. The black man is the great equalizer to leveling the playing field for today's youth. I have witnessed on many occasions the presence of strong men positively impacting the lives of young boys. Why are we not doing more?

We can no longer sit idle in hope that others do for our children what we need to bring to fruition. We must not continue to be content with our heads buried and believe that our children are not in a dismal state of being. In America, more than 1.2 million students drop out of high school and the percentage of those is staggering for black males. We, as black males, have failed to educate, provide and direct our young black males into academia. Our parents pushed us to be educated because they were very much cognizant of the obstacles that awaited us, and this push came from many parents who had less than a high school diploma.

Historically and traditionally, a black male figure was prevalent in many homes, and their mere presence made families complete. It was that male who was revered despite his flaws and imperfections. Most of the men were hard workers, and they depended on their wives to direct and nurture the family. It is amazing how parents then could raise ten kids in a two-room house and parents today cannot raise two kids in a ten-room house.

It is a moral imperative that black men once again comprehend the essence of man is his ability to change. The change I speak of is the ability that man has to change the direction in which our young black males sojourn. We must take an active role to help our young males traverse the complexities of life to take their rightful place in society – their rightful place at the top.

As I look back on my life and see what I have accomplished, I can unequivocally state that there were four black men who helped shape my character, mold my personality and communicate the importance of being a strong black man.

They instilled in me a sense of pride for my heritage and taught me to always hold my head high and only bow it to pray, while never allowing anybody to wrest away my integrity. Even though these men were from different stations in life, they all took a vested interest in me to pass on that which was so freely given to them. It was of no importance to them or me if they did or did not have a degree from some college. The point is they demonstrated a moral obligation to help me become who I am today. And, we as black males, must exhibit the same moral obligation to our young black males. We see our young boys becoming a dying commodity and yet we are allowing it. Unless you have lived under a rock for the past twenty years, you know there is credence to what I am saying.

Last, we must stop making excuses for not doing all that is necessary to rescue our black boys from a fate that will be the antithesis of what they deserve. A life without hope is merely an existence. We are witnessing the second Middle Passage against black people but only this time, the abduction is being perpetrated on our youth. Black males must rise up and establish a movement to counteract the hopelessness that will be placed upon the shoulders of this and the next generation. We owe them our time, our effort and our guidance.

"Come to the edge," He said.
They said, "We are afraid."
"Come to the edge," He said.
They came, he pushed them and they FLEW.
– Guillaume Apollinaire

Chapter Seventeen

Mentors Make a Difference

In the scriptures we are able to witness the perfect mentor, Jesus Christ. Jesus taught and mentored his disciples. And Jesus also had a mentor ...

Sydney Jordan

Public School Mentor 100

Black Men of Chicago

Mentors have played a key role in my life as a youth and even to this day. Through my life experiences, I have come to learn that these mentors were critical, especially during times of transition. This document will capture my life experiences and the effect mentors have had during particular transitions. I will follow with a recommendation of purposeful mentorship for students as young as eight years old or third grade through grade twelve.

Verily, verily, I say unto you, The Son can do nothing of himself, but what he seeth the Father do; for what things soever he doeth, these also doeth the Son likewise. (John 5:19)

I was raised in a family of twelve, including my parents. We had a home in Maywood, Illinois, a suburb just west of the city of Chicago. I was the youngest of ten children and the seventh boy. When my parents brought me home from the hospital, my older siblings were all asked who would volunteer to live with my grandparents in Raymond, Mississippi. My mom and dad spoke about how great it would be and the individual attention would be given to the person who accepts the offer. My brother Jimmy immediately raised his hand and volunteered to leave his six brothers and three sisters to live with my grandparents. Jimmy is the fifth child and the third boy in the Jordan family. He was only seven years old at the time. Jimmy's decision proved to be key for me in my later years.

I attended Irving Elementary School in Maywood School District 89. Irving is a K-8 school building. Therefore, I started as a kindergartner and went through eighth grade in this one building. All nine of my siblings attended this school except for Jimmy.

I do not remember much about my younger years, but one thing I remember like it was yesterday was the death of my dear mother on February 19, 1971. I was in second grade at the time. My family guarded me during this tragic moment in our lives to the point that I thought my mom was sleeping. I really did not fully comprehend what was happening to me and our family.

Our community was like Mayberry from the *Andy Griffin Show*. Everyone knew each other. Therefore, it was big news in the area about my mom's passing. People were very consoling and expressed their condolences. The school principal and the teachers all wondered how the family would fare with nine children at home and just the dad to take care of them all.

My aunt wanted to take the three youngest children. Despite the challenge he would face, my dad decided to not split up the family and kept us all together. My older brothers and sisters took on the maternal and paternal responsibilities to assist my dad. My dad worked two and sometimes three jobs to support the family.

Age of Accountability: Third-Sixth Grades (8-11)

The death of my mom seemed to take a toll on my brothers. Mom kept peace in the home and ensured the children were all respectful to others. However, with her passing, my oldest brother quit his great-paying job as an electrician and started running the streets. He started down the path of drugs and alcohol, which eventually took his life. The second oldest brother picked up and moved to California immediately after graduating high school. He lives there to this day. Jimmy was the least affected due to him being raised by our grandparents.

The next two brothers got into much mischief. They became well known in the community as tough guys. As a young child, I looked up to them because no one would mess with them or me. They smoked and drank, and seemed to have cool friends. They listened to great music and their bedrooms in our basement were filled with black light posters and strobe lights. I wanted to be just like them. I was headed down this path until another tragedy struck.

At age 11, our house caught fire and burned down. I was sleeping on the living room couch when it occurred. My oldest brother had just arrived home and noticed a crackling sound on the back porch. He peered out the back door window and saw the flames. We were all able to evacuate the home with no injuries. However, we were left without a home.

My dad was dating someone at the time our house burned down, and she invited our family to move in with her family and share the apartment. She had six children of her own. However, only three were still living in the apartment at the time. The five youngest children from my family moved into the apartment. This apartment was on the west side of Chicago. It was a miracle we were all able to live in the moderately sized apartment. The two brothers whom I referred to earlier as being rough guys did not live there for long. They soon found their own places and became independent, and dropped out of high school.

It was a blessing in disguise as I now had a mother who could look out for me and my other brother and sister. It was in this new neighborhood, through a mentor, that I discovered my basketball skills.

Our apartment was a block away from Columbus Park. Activities at the park in those days were aplenty for the youth. There were volunteers who organized dancing for the girls and basketball for the boys. Howard Brown was my first positive mentor. I was able to forget the tragedy that had just occurred in my life through playing organized basketball at the park district. Howard would walk seven to eight miles a day to get to the park and organize basketball practices and games around the city for the boys in my community. I am forever grateful for Howard for taking the time to do this for the boys.

Despite moving to the west side of Chicago, I continued to attend school in Maywood. After completing eighth grade, I attended Proviso East High School in Maywood. It was like living two separate lives as I went back and forth from school to home each day.

During my teen years, my dad was truly a mentor. He was a man of few words. I appreciated him keeping the family together. He also emulated the way I should work to provide for my family. My dad was also self-reliant. He grew and cultivated a garden filled with a variety of vegetables.

Earlier, I wrote about my brother Jimmy volunteering to live with our grandparents and how that proved to be beneficial for me. Over the years, I would get to see Jimmy each summer. Sometimes we went to Mississippi or he came to Chicago to visit us. I admired Jimmy. He was smart, funny and just an all-around great person. He was the only person amongst my siblings to attend and graduate from college. I wanted to be just like him.

One time, Jimmy visited us after he had graduated from college and enlisted in the Army. He spoke about the fraternity he joined in college and that the fraternity's headquarters were in Chicago. I went with him and one of my other brothers to find the Alpha house headquartered on Martin Luther King Drive. We drove around but could not locate the house. He suddenly spotted a car that he recognized. He told my brother to follow the car. Sure enough, the car parked in front of the Alpha house on King Drive. Jimmy got out of the car and embraced the gentlemen as if they were best friends, even though they had just met for the first time. This was very strange to me. It was something about the way these young men represented themselves that made me take notice. I said to myself, "I want to join this fraternity someday." The fraternity was Alpha Phi Alpha.

Jimmy gave me advice for college. He told me to have fun, but stay focused on my studies. Jimmy was no longer accessible to me because the U.S. Army took him overseas to serve. Therefore, I had to seek out others to be a mentor and guide for me.

One mentor was Greg, who now serves as my insurance

agent. Greg was only a year or two older than me. We were both taking business courses at Southern Illinois University-Carbondale. Greg gave me advice on which classes to take, which instructors to select or avoid, and not to drop classes if I could avoid it. I followed his advice and it helped me to graduate on time. When I went for advising just prior to graduation, the university advisors were surprised to see my progress having never come to her for guidance over the years.

Another mentor was Dr. Richard Gartner, who is still very active in mentoring youth to this day. Dr. Gartner was a member of Alpha Phi Alpha Fraternity. He gave me the confidence to pledge to become a member of the fraternity. Once I became a member, Dr. Gardner groomed me for leadership in the fraternity both at the local level and at the state level.

Another mentor during my college days and beyond was John Kendall. John is also a member of the Alpha Phi Alpha Fraternity. He was also raised on the west side of Chicago. His half-brother was one of my good friends in high school and college. John was a few years older than us, and he provided guidance to us while he attended school in Ohio; he even visited the Southern Illinois campus on occasions.

Upon graduating from college, I received employment in Houston with Foley's Department Stores as an Assistant Group Sales Manager (AGSM). This position was a prelude for the Group Sales Manager (GSM) position. GSMs were area managers over departments in the merchandise retail stores.

When it was time for me to become GSM, Vern Swisher, an African American store manager, asked me to head up his children's department. Mr. Swisher was a great role model. He was the only black store manager in the company. His store was one of the largest and most successful stores in the department chain. Mr. Swisher became my mentor, and I patterned myself after him. He was one of the first to arrive to the store each day, but I began to beat him to work each day. This really impressed Mr. Swisher. I quickly became one of the top GSMs in his store and was soon recruited to another store. My retail journey went through Cleveland and Columbus, Ohio before I moved back to the Chicago area to pursuing a career in educational publishing.

As soon as I moved back to the Chicago area, John Kendall asked me to attend the 100 Black Men of Chicago's mentoring program at a school in Chicago Public Schools. I later found myself involved and eventually co-directing the mentoring program. I did all of this prior to becoming a member of the organization. I just enjoyed working with the youth and giving back as a mentor. The school was located in the community where I was raised. I became a member after the fact and was awarded new member of the year for my efforts.

As part of the mentoring program, we took the boys on field trips and visited colleges. On occasion, we would bring in guests who represented a variety of careers. We held the boys accountable for their grades, good behavior and being respectful. We had them learn vocabulary words from the SAT/ACT (use in sentences, know definition, etc.). They wrote papers on different meaningful topics to present to the team. This gave the boys public speaking experience. There was a culminating event each year at the 100 Black Men of Chicago Gala. A couple of the boys were selected to introduce award winners. All the boys were dressed in tuxedos and escorted guests to their seats. This event was a time to showcase the boys and allow them the time to shine. We also encouraged the boys to network, give firm handshakes, make eye contact and ask for business cards. They later followed up with their new contacts.

I did not realize the impact of this purposeful mentoring until I ran into one of the mentees several years later. He was with his mother at a Target store. I did not recognize him at first. He had grown about a foot. He was now standing six feet, nine inches tall. I did not recognize his face, but he recognized me. He was so excited to see me. He told me that he was just talking to his mother about John and me. He told me that John and I changed his life, and had it not been for us mentoring him in the seventh and eighth grades, he had no idea where he would be today. He had just graduated with a degree and a successful basketball career from Wilberforce University of Ohio. He was headed overseas to play professional basketball.

This same year, I was able to connect with many of the

other boys (and girls) whom we mentored. All of the mentees graduated high school and attended and/or graduated college. One of the boys who struggled with his studies in elementary and high school is now pursuing a successful career in the military. This is tremendous.

Recommendation

In the scriptures we are able to witness the perfect mentor, Jesus Christ. Jesus taught and mentored his disciples. And Jesus also had a mentor. We learn this when He said, "Verily, verily, I say unto you, The Son can do nothing of himself, but what he seeth the Father do; for what things soever he doeth, these also doeth the Son likewise" (John 5:19).

Jesus is also the Great Emulator! We, in turn, have been asked to emulate Him; "What manner of men ought ye to be? Verily, I say unto you, even as I am" (3 Nephi 27:27 from the Book of Mormon).

The ways that we can emulate Jesus is by mentoring others as He did. Consider the conversation Philip had with an angel in the Book of Acts, *"And the angel of the Lord spake unto Philip, saying, Arise, and go....And he arose and went: and behold, a man of Ethiopia, an eunuch of great authority under Cadance queen of the Ethiopians, who had the charge of all her treasure, and had come to Jerusalem for to worship, Was returning, and sitting in his chariot read Esaias the prophet, Then the Spirit said unto Philip, Go near, and join thyself to his chariot. And Philip ran thither to him, and heard him read the prophet Esaias, and said, Understandest thou what thou readest? And he said, How can I, except some man should guide me?"* This is what our youth are asking us to do and it is our responsibility to be like Jesus and Philip in this example and guide our youth.

Based on my experiences and through the mentoring I have rendered firsthand, I believe mentoring should be purposefully done. The most consistent agent in the lives of our youth is the school system. This is where mentoring should be focused. My recommendation is for schools and community members to create guidance counseling/advising programs for adult males to act as mentoring agents. The youth need consistent mentors in their lives whom they trust and who will not judge them but rather guide them in love. A guidance counselor will oversee a cohort of youth starting at grade three and follow this cohort through grade twelve. The relationship built over these years will be natural for the mentor/mentee to keep through college and well into adulthood. I believe this is a simple yet effective way to ensure our youth have consistent, trustworthy guides in their lives. Youth need someone to keep them on track in school and to provide counsel and a listening ear. This will give them a blueprint of what they can be by exposing them to positive options. A journal article by Michael Karcher entitled, *Increases in Academic Connectedness and Self-Esteem Among High School Students Who Serve as Cross-Age Peer Mentors,* concluded that when mentees reach high school, they should be encouraged to be peer mentors to elementary students (Karcher, 2009). They should also be encouraged to give back as volunteer mentors post high school. I believe that this type of purposeful mentoring will be the key to strengthening families and producing successful youth academically and personally. Thus, communities as a whole will be strengthened.

Chapter Eighteen

Blessings of the Village

My hope is for the African American males who are in education serving as teachers and school leaders to share their experiences with our young males.

Dr. Darnell Bell

Elementary Principal

By favor, I married the most amazing woman in the world. Just looking at her daily inspires me to be the best that I can be. We have four wonderful children, who are our life, and who we protect and love dearly. My life story has been filled with many ups and downs, twists and turns, and hills to climb. But through it all, God has ALWAYS been there for me. There were, and still are on occasion, times when I think God is nowhere to be found. However, the simple truth is that He was, and is always carrying me through his SON Jesus Christ. I constantly thank God for His guidance by the Holy Spirit, during the most difficult times of my life. I am not perfect, nor do I profess to be; but I am a saved sinner by the grace of God through Jesus Christ. A song by Bryan Courtney Wilson has a lyric that says, "One man can't tell the story." Well, this is where my journey begins to add to the collection of the stories.

My life's journey began on June 6, 1970, in the early hours of the morning in Los Angeles, California. My birth parents Mildred Fegans and Willie George Bell, never played a significant role in my life. In my youth I lived in California, while my birth mother lived in Arkansas. I have always wanted to ask my birth mother why she left me, or better yet, why she did not participate in my life.

As my birth mother continued on her journey in Arkansas, and my birth father continued on his in California, God blessed me with two individuals who became my mom and dad. Doris Weaver (Mama Doris) and Luke Weaver (Daddy Luke) raised me. Despite raising their five children, they took on the task of raising two of their grandchildren, Pop and Trelle. If you are wondering, my nickname is Pop.

While living in Los Angeles, I had a strong network of support from my aunts and uncles. Even though they had children of their own, they ALWAYS treated and considered me as one of their own. One particularly special moment I remember vividly was when one of my uncles accompanied his son, my cousin and me to a father-and-son event at the school. The reason this memory sticks out to me is because internally that was the first time I wondered why weren't my biological parents involved in my life. Why couldn't I have a father who wanted to be involved in his son's life, like my uncle was involved in his son's life? I never really heard anyone talk about my father and mother. One of my aunts told me that my mom left me a letter saying that she was going to come back for me.

While living in Los Angeles, I attended Forty-Ninth Street Elementary School until the second grade. I really loved attending that school because children of all races and nationalities were represented there. School was fun, interesting and very hands-on. The school was located in South Central, Los Angeles in the center of gang activity. Being raised in Los Angeles for the first seven years of my life afforded me the opportunity of seeing things that I would never have imagined seeing. I witnessed gang activity up close and personal; from the blue and red bandanas, gang graffiti, gang violence, and hearing and seeing the aftermath of drive-by shootings.

But I really believe that most of my scars occurred after I left California in the summer of 1977. My security blanket was ripped away from me. Mama Doris, Trelle and I began my second leg of my journey in a small town named Stephens, Arkansas. This is where I began to see the world in Black and White. This is where I first heard about racism and people experiencing being prejudice because of the color of their skin. This was is also the first time I met my biological mother. While in California I never spoke about my mom to anyone but Aunt Beverly. When we did, she gave me a scripture from Psalm 27:10: "When my father and my mother forsake me; then the Lord will take me up!"

When I met my mother, I thought, "How am I supposed to feel? She is not my mama; my mama is Mama Doris." Wow, as I reflect on that moment now, what a bombshell. How was I supposed to feel about a woman I never developed a motherly bond with? All I knew was that as a baby or toddler, we visited Arkansas, and she returned back to California with us. She eventually left again without me, and returned to Arkansas. I hadn't seen her until this moment. I had no recollection of her, no type of feelings for her, and don't even remember seeing a photograph of her. I found out that she was married, and that I had a sister. Mama Doris would always say, "That is your mother," and I would constantly say, "No, she is not – YOU ARE!"

Year after year would pass with empty promises from my biological mother. She would promise to buy me school clothes, toys and gifts for birthdays and Christmas, but all those promises turned out to be empty. Did I ask to be here? Did I ask you to introduce yourself to me as my mother? Did I ask you to do anything for me? The resounding answer was NO. She continued to tear my heart into pieces as I continued to get my hopes up that she would finally come through on her promises. I would lie to people when they asked what my biological mom got me for my birthday or for Christmas. I would tell them that she said she was going to buy me something in a few days. Year after year, I would see my sister with new clothes and things around income tax time, and the only thing I received from her were more empty promises. The only father I knew died when I was in the fifth grade, so we returned back to California for my fifth grade year.

At the beginning of my junior high school years, I became very interested in sports and band. My basketball coach, band director and science teacher, all who happened to be African American males, became strong role models in my life. Not only did they insist on me doing my best in school, they created environments where sports and music was used to teach about life. They were my mentors throughout my junior high and high school years. Every obstacle in my life that I had to overcome, God placed strong Christian individuals in my life to guide me through the storms of life.

After high school, I successfully completed two bachelor's degrees, a master's program, and a doctoral degree. I have been divorced and remarried. I entered the field of education as a fifth grade teacher in the Little Rock School District in December of 1999. I served as a fifth grade teacher and instructional coach for nine years in that district. I am currently serving as a principal in the Pulaski County Special School District.

People enter into education for a variety of reasons, but my reason for entering into this field is because a calling was placed on my life from God. For the past thirteen years, I have witnessed firsthand the state of our young African American boys in our public school system, and the importance of them having strong, Christian, African American role models in the schools. Our African American boys are struggling with a plethora of issues including low self-esteem, lack of anger management skills and poor academic achievement, just to name a few. My hope is for African American males in education serving as teachers and school leaders to share their experiences with our young males. Our young males need to see that we share similar stories; face the same obstacles, and can overcome whatever situation life may have thrown at them. They need to realize that it is not where you came from, but where you are going.

As I look back over my life, I now realize that God has provided me with a great story, or testimony, to use to mentor boys in the buildings I serve. It's time for us as African American educators, leaders and men to step up to assist with the development of our boys academically as well as teaching them how to become men. It's time for black men to wake up, stand up, speak up, and be the strong, Christian black men God intended us to be.

Chapter Nineteen

The Power of Love

Students need to see role models who have used education to get ahead and in turn, there will be more people like Ben Carson and his gifted hands all over this nation.

Saleem Osman Bilal

In thinking about my experience as a father raising four black males, I cannot help but think about the experiences that shaped my life. Fatherhood was just a part of the family unit. Fatherhood is equal parts instinct, group association and environmental influence.

Mothers, to me, are the essence of the family unit through which everything flows. They are essential to a healthy family. I believe that black mothers and fathers around my age – particularly those whose parents and grandparents migrated from the south in the 1920s, 1930s and 1940s – had similar experiences growing up.

The family unit, for the most part, consisted of two parents with many children from that union. Also included were cousins, uncles, aunts and grandparents. My neighborhood and the surrounding neighborhoods were all the same – overflowing with families just like mine!

In each of the family units, the father was the central authority, even though he was home the least. He was usually at work and came home in the evenings. There were many television shows during those days that centered on family life and the daily family situations. Shows such as Leave it to Beaver, Father Knows Best, The Donna Reed Show and many others depicted family situations that we all could relate to and enjoyed watching.

Then, there was the public school system, which seemed to be an extension of the home. Concepts about the family and its function were everywhere. It seemed like everything was preparing you to be a parent.

I experienced a pretty normal upbringing. I was born in St. Louis, Missouri, in the 1950s. The neighborhood I grew up in had everything that a model community should have in it – small confectionery stores, supermarkets, drug stores, a high school, elementary schools, a small hospital named in honor of an African American, a community center, fire department and a host of other amenities. All of these structures were within walking distance of my house.

I had six brothers and sisters, and cousins galore. The first eight years or so I was at home with my mother and family, then after that I was sent to live with my grandmother who lived about six blocks away. I never figured out why, but all I know is it could not have worked out better.

My grandmother had six children and all of them had at least two children, with some of them having as many as seven. And since they all would come by to see "Big Mother," they would bring their children, which meant I had plenty of time to play with my cousins.

It also put me in the unique position of getting to know many of my grandmother's contemporaries. I sat with my elders and listened to their views on life. As a child growing up, the rule was that you could be seen but not heard. Since I was a very obedient child, I never got out of line while she sat with her friends.

Most of the values I have today came from a combination of all of the above, with my grandmother contributing the common sense portion. Her love of God always was displayed in her manner. She always wanted me to put God first in all my life's choices and taught me how to do so in various ways. She wanted me to have a better education than her generation. Her own education only went through the third grade but in terms of understanding human behavior and wisdom, she had a Ph.D.

She knew that a good education without morals or the desire to do right and treat people with respect would not lead to being a good human being. She wanted me to be a person who was fair and loved everyone. I know that is why she was the central figure in our family because of her value and respect for each person she met.

She never looked down on anyone; instead, she was more like a servant to all without being servile. Her temperament was next to saintliness; she never lost her temper, and it would hurt you more to see her disappointed in you for something you did than for her to lose her temper and whoop you! I loved her so much that it was an honor to have lived with her. I ate simple meals beside her, I slept next to her, I went to church with her and I watched television with her. And when the time was right, she would let me find my own way.

So, armed with the influence of her ways, I stumbled through adolescence, constantly hearing her voice reminding me to always do what is right. As I said earlier, the public school was an extension of the home. I did not realize how valuable that experience was until I was older. The dedicated teachers I had in the public schools had a huge impact on my life. The way it was back then, the female teachers taught the lower grades and the male teachers took over after you reached seventh grade. Teachers ranged from being very motherly to firm disciplinarians.

Then, it was on to junior high where we encountered the tough, authoritative male figures. They really wanted you to succeed, so there was no sympathy or excuse for failing to make an all-out effort in your studies. Male teaching figures were really valuable. They commanded respect in the home; they were honored by our parents and the neighborhood in general. It seemed everyone was on the same page, and the family looked out for you and the neighbors would also look out for the teachers. Even your fellow students would keep an eye on you and "tell" if you were caught misbehaving or acting out.

After I received my coveted high school diploma, I was set to pursue a degree in business. This is where I stumbled. College required discipline, which I did not have at the time. I could have used some good advice around then but being young and hard-headed, I probably would not have listened anyway. However, I still could have used some. Since I did not have a degree or a marketable skill, securing a good job was very difficult. But, because of my upbringing and values, I was always able to find work doing various jobs. I have always valued learning and knowledge, so libraries and bookstores were my second home. I honestly can say this was instilled in me through my parents and the efforts of family members and school leaders.

There are just no words to describe the feeling of learning something. I am sure this is why my wife appealed to me so much. She was intense about learning, even more so than me. We met in high school, and I had no idea that she would be my future wife. It was not until I moved away to New York that I became serious about family life. So, since she and I had a friendship already, we shared some of our thoughts on the kind of children we wanted to bring into society. As it turned out, we had much in common and continue to some forty years later.

We married and then moved to New York. This was the 1970s and 1980s, a time for Black awareness. We had three of our children during this era, and they all got a dose of what it was like to be Black in America at that time. It was an amazing time. There were so many activities for community growth and development, and people everywhere were joining in. This also was a time for the hippie movement, inclusion movement and empowering the people movement. It really was an exciting time, and I think my sons inherited the spirit of awareness and desire to learn as a result.

My sons learned this spirit from her because she had it instilled in her from the previous generation. She had a love for the African American spirit of our ancestors, and she did everything to keep that spirit alive and growing in them. We also embraced Al Islam at an early age, which fueled our love for truth, justice and equality. She used everything as a teaching tool to prepare our children with this spirit. From home schooling to public schooling, she walked every step of the way with them to ensure their success.

All three of the older children have college degrees, but their degrees are not their most valuable assets – it is their values as human beings that make me most proud. My grandmother would be proud of them because they are men of substance who stand for truth, honor and dignity. In addition, I know if you tried to give my wife or I credit for helping them become the men they are, we all would say on behalf of the previous generations, "It takes a village."

In closing, what are my hopes? My hopes are to see the black male student develop fervor for learning just as our ancestors did when they were at last given the opportunity to learn to read. It is reported in history that the eagerness to learn how to read by the ex-slaves was so strong that little children were seen teaching adults and the elderly how to read. In turn, the adults were so happy to learn that they would be seen in the wee hours of the night reading by candlelight!

If our youth would again develop this love and enthusiasm for learning, our public school issue would cease to exist. We need more black male teachers participating in the system. Students need to see role models who have used education to get ahead and in turn, there will be more people like Ben Carson and his gifted hands all over this nation.

However, all of this must start at home with mothers, fathers, neighbors and communal support. My hope is that we turn off the television, read more and continue to achieve!

Chapter Twenty

The Time Is Now

Public schools have become holding cells –
holding a generation of young brothers captive
until they walk out into the "free" at age 18,
totally unprepared, and reading at an eighth grade
or below level, with no transferable skills.

Dr. Michael W. Nellums

Over forty years ago, a great American songwriter wrote the words to the song "Lean On Me." Alone in a world vastly different from the one he grew up in, and deeply troubled, he chose to reflect back on his roots in a rural community where he "knew" that in times of crisis or difficulty, someone had his back. He knew others were there to support him and provide an uplifting hand during his time of greatest need.

Four decades later, that song and all it represents appears to be lost with adult black males supporting young black males in public schools. It is as removed from the psyche of adult black men as the memory of the dreaded "middle passage" of our forefathers. The phrase "for better or worse" represents a set of words commonly used in a commitment ceremony in our country. As African American men, the abandonment of this commitment is all too familiar with our families, especially our sons. As black men of African descent, we must accept the latter as our reality for the current state of being of young black males in the educational system. Using any measuring tool to chart historical progress, African American boys are in worse shape than ever in public schools across this country. At the same time, African American men have gone totally MIA (missing in action) in the educational upbringing of their sons, their legacies and their namesakes.

The token appearances made on Friday nights for basketball and football games do not add up to any real degree of responsibility. By then, it's too late. The mold has been cut; the die has been cast. By middle school, the young brothers are reading three grades behind. By high school, they're four grades behind and scoring ten to fifteen points lower than their white male counterparts on the ACT, and several hundred points lower on the SAT. They are getting credit for signing their names, and then they are lost. The system of public education put into place to provide these young black boys with a free and appropriate education will shortly exhibit its greatest moral failure. Black boys on average will score lower than every other ethnic group on these standardized exams. Pre-K through twelfth grade will become the lost years.

Yes, that means that on average, many African American youth, especially males, score in the single digits on ACT exams. That disparity increases even further on most state proficiency exams. Their glory on the game court and athletic fields does not overcome their profound and highly measured inadequacies in the classrooms. They are simply LEFT BEHIND.

Perhaps No Child Left Behind (NCLB) should have been called Black Boys Always Left Behind (BBALB). It appears today from any view – straight-ahead, peripheral or through rose-colored glasses – young black boys are not closing any academic gaps. And yes, black folks are as much to blame as anyone else.

To illustrate the urgency of their situation, I would like for you to digest these facts. Forty-two percent of all African American boys enrolled in public schools have failed an entire grade at least once and only 18 percent of all black men ages 20-21 are enrolled in college. Across this country, unemployment rates among young black men exceed 50 percent as jobs have left many urban areas. This remains true in my state and metropolitan area as well. No Child Left Behind, the most comprehensive education reform action of our lifetime, has had no significant impact on the high school graduation rates for black males, which is consistently less than 50 percent in most major urban areas. I have a son who is not in that number. He was a solid high school student and became a college graduate. I am blessed. He didn't become a negative statistic because we followed a plan of preparation for his life in the public school arena.

When our son was a toddler, we read to him daily to increase his exposure to language and to increase his vocabulary. We made him practice writing and exposed him to art. We planned, watched and intervened. We exposed him to positive images of black people and refused to accept average grades when we knew he could and would live up to our expectations, and not down to theirs.

I have the professional pleasure of serving on the school board of the largest district in the state I call home. Although the board of education can be time consuming, I know that my service matters. Arthur Ashe once said that. "From what we get, we can make a living; what we give, however makes a life." I know black boys need a real advocate in the leadership and decision making position in public schools outside of the local building. They need someone who understands policy, politics and most important, "Equity and Equitable." Not equal, or even, but equitable.

African American boys are doing so poorly in most of our city schools in Little Rock that their testing scores only reach 50 percent proficiency in one testing area, elementary math. When this sobering statistic was shared to a majority African American board, there was no public outrage, no righteous indignation. I alone appeared to express dismay. After my comments, another African American male board member made a few comments. I then expressed my profound disappointment and inquired about the district's plan of action. Five other board members, including two additional African Americans, were largely silent. A patron of the district told me that it appeared that only two people cared: the two African American males on the board. However, with this fact now in the public domain, the presenter did not pause, nor have any unusual inflections in his voice that would normally indicate uneasiness in sharing such disappointing news. It felt like everyone should have expected this kind of disturbing news. We should not be angry or discouraged. "It's just the way things are." Get over it.

There was no visible reaction from the board president. She did not shake her head nor appear to be distressed. However, she had no real reason to – her children were enrolled in private schools. Interestingly, she sat as school board president of an urban, majority-minority school district. This oxymoron itself warrants another book. The superintendent, who was a really conscientious brother, did not make any "you-can-expect-radical-changes-ahead promises." It was just business as usual. The overall lack of concern displayed by the administration, the board, and parents of these children was an obvious indicator that nothing more was expected and no consequences would follow. Below is a snapshot of what was presented to the board of directors after state testing in 2011.

Little Rock Public Schools				
Percent Proficient	African American Males	Caucasian Males	African American Males	Caucasian Males
Elementary Schools District	52%	87%	43%	80%
Middle Schools District	Math 40%	86%	Literacy 40%	84%
High Schools District	Algebra 43%	70%	11th Grade Literacy 43%	78%
Central High	48%	72%	31%	88%

These scores represent the disparate academic gaps that increase at every level district-wide from elementary to middle school. In high school, black boys fare no better and at our flagship program that each year touts at least one National Merit Scholar. At our world renowned Central High School, African American male proficiency rates were 57 percentage points below white males in eleventh grade literacy. Quoting Morgan Freeman, from the movie, *Lean On Me:* "That means they can hardly read!"

Roughly six years ago as a middle school principal, I requested a meeting with the Assistant Superintendent for Instruction, the Assistant Superintendent of Desegregation, the Assistant Superintendent for Human Resources, and the Monitor from the Office of Desegregation. The latter was there as a matter of supposed equity for students of color. I asked for this meeting because my school was largely

African American, male, and low-achieving with pronounced deficiencies in language arts and math. We were 90 percent free and reduced lunch and thus qualified for approximately $400,000 worth of supplemental educational funding with money from a funding source known as the NSLA. With that additional income, I wanted to hire math and English teachers to tutor a group of students after school who were poor, largely African American, and low achieving. After numerous intentional delays, the meeting was eventually held. We sat at the table. I was on one side, and all other parties on the other. It became an assault on the alleged condition of African American boys and "what they could do without." Folks of African American descent that knew the condition of these boys started telling me that, the program was not necessary, and the teachers were doing a good job. I listened as an African American woman and two African American men told me that the need was not great enough to justify that type of expenditure. One well spoken, obviously privileged, African American man at the table said that I asked for too much, and because of that, I was being ignored like a "squeaky wheel that constantly needed grease."

I sat at a table and listened for two hours to these dream killers. I listened to a charlatan persuade three other African American men and women that a tutoring program for African American boys and girls who were scoring less than 20 percent on standardized state math and literacy test was a bad idea. The sixth grade African American math scores on the Standardized Arkansas Benchmark exam topped out at a whopping 4 percent. That's right – 96 percent of those black boys didn't pass sixth grade math, and one of their teachers was the local president of the teachers' union. You see, it is our fault too. We are silent partners to the destructive actions of others against our sons.

I am always deeply troubled when I see deceptive academic statements and statistics coming from those who know better or should know the truth about the progress of young black boys in public schools. I compare it to buying and then selling spoiled fruit, like a rotten banana or apple. You look at the outer skin and it still has some color, but if you observe it closely and squeeze it ever so slightly, you feel and recognize the rot is coming from the core. The inner portion – the heart and soul of these young brothers – is wasting away.

This is significant because the powers that be are trying to reclaim spoiled fruit instead of planting new trees. It is this let's-raise-the-whole-school-score approach that has allowed young black males to literally rot away in the same classroom that embraces and propels the high achievers, yet sutures the deeply wounded and distressed. What the public sees is an incomplete picture, one that is presented as rosy, even when it's dark and distressing. African American parents are often presented school wide statistics that show minimal improvement. The truth is a large percentage of students from low-income families continue to underperform and in many cases regress, from year to year.

Education is supposed to be the great equalizer, yet this gap between the economically disadvantaged and the economically affluent continues to grow. Tragically young African American boys are at the forefront of this "Great American Tragedy." As young African American boys grow into African American men, they often take no transferrable skills. They cannot verbalize, they cannot write, they cannot do math, and they have limited technology skills – all as a result of the public school system. They become casualties of what should be a war to say the least, but which has rapidly become "a tale of schools within a school"; often under the same roof, but vastly separate and unequal.

I recall these words like yesterday. "As long as he keeps his head on his desk and remains quiet, I do not have a problem just passing him," said the apathetic teacher. As a young African American male teaching in the educational system I was appalled, highly offended and discouraged. I went into a I-must-save-all-the-black-boys mode. I asked that she allow the student to be transferred to my class. Privately, I wish I could have pushed her out of the school house door and into that child's shoes for a walk through his poverty-ridden neighborhood.

Across this country, these individuals are all too familiar with urban classrooms serving lower-income to "downright po" African American students. In my eyes, this person was nothing short of a highly compensated assassin, and in urban school environments, more often than not, the real victims are the young black boys. Their lives become "a dream unfulfilled."

I've worked with a few of those assassins in my day. As a principal, I had an English teacher who failed multiple groups of largely black male students, twice in the same year. She would fail them once during a semester, and then she would teach summer school where they had to enroll, and they would fail again. The fix was in. She had a plan to employ herself and to make extra compensation by teaching summer school every year to this group of failing black male students. This is the kind of game that young black boys are exposed to in public schools all across the country. She reminded me of Erwinia bacteria, a type of bacteria that causes "soft rot" in vegetables. It gets in through bruises on the surface, and eventually causes the vegetables to turn to mush.

That is exactly how young brothers are beaten down. They're bruised by a lack of success in the classroom, and then one career killer digs in, and pummels and pummels until the skin breaks. In this case, what breaks is the young brother's will. He loses his will to keep fighting where there is no real love. He loses his will to work, to assimilate and to find his own identity. He then searches for it wherever he can find it. This is not a dream deferred, but the beginning of a permanent nightmare.

In middle and high schools all across this country, hope has plainly been removed from the psyche of young black boys. Failure does not appear optional. News of male African American academic achievement is largely negative, with a few goodwill stories sprinkled here and there called isolated success. However, when 80 percent of all middle school eighth grade African American boys across the country are reading at fourth grade levels, the time for radical action is overdue. The inferior quality of education being delivered in many urban schools has the most damaging long-term effect on young brothers and their communities. These negatives become major factors in the creation of a permanent underclass.

Amid this sad state of affairs, African American men have become Silent Sams. Disowning any real responsibility to take care of their own, they have effectively abandoned black boys in public schools. Literally speaking, at crunch time African American men have called a timeout and pulled themselves out of the game. Call them what you may – detached, aloof, disinterested, unconcerned, or indifferent – it's all applicable. Black men have ostensibly deserted that mantra, of "lean on me" for these young brothers. Subsequently, they have allowed unqualified substitutes to step in and call the last play of the most important game these young black men will ever play: LIFE.

According to an old African proverb, "Blind belief is dangerous." Life often produces moments where our beliefs are not only challenged but put to the ultimate test. I am often reminded that African Americans own very few media outlets (newspapers, print magazines, radio and TV stations). Fear and uncertainty, or false hope and outright lies, are mass produced and applied disproportionally toward the black community.

That fictitious message and unrealistic portrait is one that is consumed daily about the well-being and progress of young black boys in urban and rural schools across this country. It is a sham perpetrated on folks who lack institutional knowledge and real facts supported by data.

I have always been accused of speaking too much truth. I am the squeaky wheel. I simply made too much noise. I demanded better facilities for poor and disadvantaged students. I demanded better teachers and learning conditions for disadvantaged students. I demanded. I did not ask. I demanded. I have lived poor, eaten free lunch, walked to school, chopped a lot of cotton, and then "got an education." Through it all, my voice has not wavered; my viewpoint has never changed. I have always looked at the factual issues of inequity, through real eyes and not through rose colored glasses.

For almost a quarter of a century, in the urban school district I called home, African American people heard rosy words from the press, the school superintendent of the moment, and the public school people at the state department. As black men, we have long trusted everyone else to save black boys, including teachers who thought that passing your African American son on to the next grade with a low C, or a lower D, was doing you a favor. This has to end. The head stone on that grave needs to read, "Lived way too long, and died 2013."

As black men, our belief in the system's ability to prepare our young black boys for "adult black man success" should always be tempered by our own frightening life experiences. Instead, we have chosen to exercise this blind faith that others know what is best for our young black boys, and they will help them reach their greatest potential. The unmitigated truth is, no one in the world can help a young black boy understand and prepare for life as a black male, but a black man. No one can recreate the struggle, hardships and systemic inequities that men of African American descent will face in their lifetimes. Transferring cultural knowledge is priceless. Getting it any other way, creates a false illusion that the world will treat you as equals. The bitterness created by a lifetime of denied opportunities will chew at the very essence of their souls. They are after all, their father's children.

The current struggle is reminiscent of slavery's dreaded Middle Passage. The oppressor never counts the human factor, the generational dynamics, and the long-term effects of uneducated subclasses of citizens. No, they simply calculate cost as a bottom line on their spreadsheet. It is though public school systems are making a blanket PA announcement:

"Regardless of your performance, I still get state tax dollars to provide you the minimum. The question becomes, can I tolerate you in a public school environment until they incarcerate you using my additional tax dollars? What is my trade-off?" I know that sounds callous, even harsh. But with so much at stake, truth is harsh and the options are few.

Let us call the public schools what they have become according to America's statistics on African American boys and crime. Public schools have become holding cells – holding a generation of young brothers captive until they walk out into the "free" at age eighteen, totally unprepared, and reading at an eighth grade or below level, with no transferable skills. I compared the plight of young black boys in public schools to the Middle Passage of Slavery. If they are not strong enough to survive a repressive society, community, and public school system, then they are thrown overboard. There is no life jacket, no swimming back to the ship. The waters are choppy, the sea is rough, the wind is fierce, and the ocean is in an absolute fury. What do these young brothers have to cling to? I call it high-priced apathy. A system of ill-equipped, non-effective educational practitioners, inclusive of school system/series of teachers/and quick-dollar consultants from anywhere but the communities and states many are born in and will die in. They do not speak like these children, or know or care to learn anything about their culture, community or history. Adding insult to injury, black men disappear completely until young black boys have exited public schools completely. No wonder young black men are exploring recreational and mind-altering drugs in alarming rates.

Two years ago, I worked at a juvenile prison where 85 percent of all those incarcerated were black boys and girls, and 75 percent were black males. This gave me new perspective. A juvenile-only facility filled with young African American men with a plethora of problems that only God could seemingly solve. Recidivism is high. Extremely low reading levels, poor verbal skills, mental health issues, and finally a prevalent history of drug abuse were the norm.

Yet, many of these boys were in no hurry to get home. They had become institutionalized. They had no real plans to re-enter the civilized world they left behind. They were satisfied to receive three meals a day, free health, vision and dental care, and to learn their rights through the prison system instead of civics class. They didn't care what was outside of the walls as long as they stayed safe inside. The state provided a safety blanket and many enjoyed the warmth.

Upon incarceration, most of the children there lost touch with their families. So distraught over the juveniles' consistent pattern of misbehavior, many of their parents never visited. An unusual observance was that African American boys relished in the power of aloneness. One would assume that they reveled in the naked independence it promotes. They didn't seem to get how the system works on the outside or in the institution. It's almost impossible for any black man or boy to be successful in the world we live in without "technical assistance." Many of these kids were classified as mentally deficient, and needed extreme counseling to address their current "life state."

Their mental health issues impaired these young African American boys to such a degree that they have become islands – while the rest of America lives exclusively on the mainland.

Prisons are built to hold and segregate a part of the population from another. Juvenile prisons focus on rehabilitating and promoting better life choices, but the young brothers in the system are so conflicted, they lack good decision-making skills. As a direct result, their negative behavior never disappears, and lies largely dormant until they can figure out a way to game the system. Within the school environment, many African American boys acted out daily. I refer to it as general disorder. It is nothing more than a series of calculated misbehaviors designed solely for the purpose of disruption. They would get up and walk out of class, turn over chairs or refuse to participate in any form of instruction. It was a drastic change for me to walk into a system that accepted lower levels of academic achievement as the norm for these incarcerated black boys. I thought prison would be the anti-societal expectation for these young black males.

The saving grace for these young black males were three campus administrators and three or four black male and female staff members who constantly preached that "this was not the life they were destined to be a part of." However, the inadequacy of the professional educators in a prison system is striking. The lower level of expectations based solely on the fact that you were teaching an "angry black male" was heartbreaking. While I try to be optimistic about most things, this very dreary picture of young black boys living in this country and underperforming in public schools, en route to a public or private prison has me vexed. I'd like to believe that race will not define nor be the predominant predictor of the successes or failures of young black boys in public schools, but every piece of state testing data and youth correctional information tells me otherwise. The total public school picture is disheartening. Yet adult black males have elected to become spectators; quick to discuss the raw deal, but largely invisible during the day-to-day operations of the public school environment. While the mother of their sons stands alone in the principal's office shedding tears for the latest disciplinary incident or academic failure, daddy fusses like hell over the cell phone, and then disappears.

The Kanuri people share with us that we must hold a true friend with both hands. The question becomes, how do we embrace the endangered species identified as young black males? Do we hold on to them with both hands or do we continue to push them into the hands of those whose interest in their preparation for future success is minimal at best and toxic at worst? These are people who obviously do not care if a young brother is unprepared, lacks assimilation skills and reads at a fourth grade level at age fifteen. Their primary concern is to take their urban school paycheck and take it back to the suburbs and spend it. They have higher priced neighborhoods to keep the undesirables out, and they don't have to drive through the streets or public housing projects that their students call home.

My own interaction has led me to this conclusion concerning African American boys in grades four to twelve. They too are discouraged about their prospects and their own potential to overcome. Their support groups are minimal; no one is there to cheer them on, not even black men.

We see lots of folks working with them, or should I say around them, trying to nudge schools up 2 percent here and 3 percent there. You know, just enough to get the school off of the state school improvement list and to pocket large sums of School Improvement money to "allegedly" make the whole school better. The simple but "inconvenient truth" is that by and large, the school improvement business is failing African American boys too. School Education Improvement Corporations have been formed to address school-wide deficiencies in urban and largely minority populated areas, which start and end with a lack of academic progress from young black males. Instead of evaluating and developing programs that specifically target black boys, the criteria to gain access into this multi-million dollar enterprise has become palm pressing, and wining and dining.

After working in a largely minority school district, one company in Arkansas billed a school district $500,000 for leadership services and produced a 10-page summary assessment for an entire year's worth of work. Meanwhile, male African American scores in this district showed no increase. Yet this waste of resources continues year after year with the same for-profit companies. When all of their improvement is done, black boys are still at the bottom, and their lack of basic skills has created a new group of millionaires.

These so-called leadership organizations have become the biggest public "Don Magic Juans" in the country. Their employee base is non-diversified, they operate with no socio-cultural concept, and they are politically connected from the top of the government through friendship, kinship, or "good ol' boy- and girl-ism." When asked for specifics, they are largely silent about successful strategies that their companies offer that target improvement with what should be the central focus of school improvement strategies: African American boys.

For young black males living in this country, the path to manhood has become a journey to Mt. Everest. Even for the most skilled navigator, it is a punishing, brutal and physically exhaustive climb. Hope and tragedy appear to be synonymous with living with brown skin. They live their entire lives knowing that someday the color of their skin will affect every opportunity they may or may not have until they cease to breathe their last breath.

Unlike many young black males today, I grew up with just as many encouragers as detractors. Like many small cities in the south, my community was governed strictly along racial lines. We had no black elected city officials, no black school administrators, no interracial churches, and almost all black people lived on the west side of the railroad tracks. My first real experience with school integration was unpleasant. We were not allowed to ride a school bus that drove past our house and therefore walked a mile to get to our new place of learning. As we left the familiarity of the neighborhood on the west side of the railroad tracks, we were greeted with racial taunts and haunting stares from the doorsteps of our white neighbors from the east side.

Some incidents in our lives are permanently woven into the very fabric of our being. It was 1970, and as a third grader going out to recess, Sharon Surge and I were the only two African American children in the "A" class. Groups were still identified by scholastic ability in that day, and there were two African American A students in the third grade. None of the white children would play with us, so we spent recess playing catch with each other and our teacher, an older white lady named, Mrs. Cobb. She put on her best face and walked us to the playground daily until she thought we could make it on our own. When that day finally arrived, Sharon and I went to play on the seesaw and were promptly greeted by the choir of Nancy Covington, Judy Perkins and Joyce Miller with a resounding chorus of "Nigger Go Home."

How does a third grader process those words? Forty years later, I still have no answer. This lack of relationship building ended when the white Baptist preacher's daughter decided that she would befriend us and play kickball. At least it became the "three of us." Compare this to a young brother struggling in the classroom with an absent father, a single mother trying to raise three other kids, and a lack of real love in his school from other adults. Paraphrasing the words of singer Natalie Cole, this child is "catching hell." Whether it is Central High of 1957, or African American eleventh graders at Central High scoring 57 percent lower on Benchmark Exams than their white male counterparts in 2011, what has really changed?

The rest of elementary became a blur. We went home for summer recess, and looked for part-time summer work chopping cotton, or if you were 13 years old, working for CETA. The white students in our town swam all day at the community swimming pool. I always thought it was a private pool like the country club. When I was 23, I learned otherwise. It was owned by the city, but operated by the Jaycees with city tax dollars and it had an open policy of discrimination. No black members were allowed even though the city paid for maintenance and general upkeep and leased the pool to the Jaycees for the grand sum of $1 a year. Wow.

I did well in school. I was always at or near the top of my class. When I was a football player in junior high,

I participated in a pep rally, and was called down by the cheerleaders to get the spirit stick. Of course, all of the cheerleaders were white, and as part of the spirit routine, I was asked to do a dance with them called the bump. Some of you may remember it as a 1970s dance that required the male and the female to bump hips in a rhythmic fashion. That was the entire motion of the dance: bumping hips.

But on this warm September day in 1975 in England, Arkansas, all hell was breaking loose behind the scenes because of my participation in the "bump dance" at the pep rally. You see, I did the bump dance with a white girl for about one whole minute, and the teachers thought the school and the community were destined for hell. It was the apocalypse they all knew would happen when we integrated schools. I was told by the only black coach we ever had in our hometown to never do that again. It was eye opening. It was just an innocent dance. But this was 1975 and we lived in south-central Arkansas. The rules, as I discovered that day, were very different. Socialization to a point and then, don't forget the color of your skin nor the context of school activities within the social backdrop of the community. I didn't know what to think, I just listened. The rest of high school life in my hometown was more of the same: two worlds with one set of rules written and enforced by those in charge. There was no black man to say, "It's ok," or "Things are going to get better." There was only one who said, "Don't ever do that again."

Today, more than thirty years later, school-age African American boys suffer silently because black men have abdicated their responsibilities as fathers, uncles, brothers, grandparents, cousins, and the like. Thirty-plus years later, black boys are languishing in this inferior state because someone keeps ignoring, refusing and passing along the "good quiet kids" or cheering and cheating for the great athletes. The African American father, uncle, cousin and brother have become defacto partners to this shameful masquerade. Too much hell is raised when a kid can't dress for a ballgame, and not enough hell is raised if the kid can't read or add up his high school credits.

I remember when reading deficiencies were identified by the Sunday school teacher. Many of you reading this book also remember that time. You were those children reading on Sunday morning. Even the kid with the stuttering problem read, and was encouraged by the Sunday School teacher and superintendent. Yes, it is still that simple to identify a seven-year-old student with a reading problem, but somehow that kid makes it to middle school and can't spell cat.

The time is now. The onus is ours. African American men cannot wait another day to collectively step up to the plate and be "partly" responsible for the successes and perceived failures of African American boys in the public education system. I anticipate the so-called black leadership being dismissive and insisting that it is society's job to help the cellar-dwelling brothers. Others will say that the public schools are failing the young brothers and the opportunities just aren't there. And finally the most shameful response, or lack thereof, will come from the "bourgeois black folks." From their seat on the sideline where they have been for the last thirty years their response will be, "I got mine, and it ain't got nothing to do with me."

The sad truth is that if you are a male of African American descent and live in the United States of America, it has everything to do with you, the future of your people and the health and well-being of the communities you choose to live in and call home. It has everything to do with the physical health of your communities, the number of unwed mothers who will dot the landscape, the crime rate in the neighborhoods you live in and the personal body and physical property attacks you are likely to witness, and be or become party to in your lifetime. It has everything to do with the number of African American males you will witness on a stage anywhere graduating from high school – or in a courtroom somewhere graduating toward prison.

The saddest part of this drama is that for those African American men and women who have daughters, it has everything to do with the future happiness and limited, or limitless, choices your daughter(s) will or will not have. I offer no apologies for my honesty because I am a realist. Although I believe in the potential of people and the human race, this is realism. We will have been effectively subjugated. Our boys will have become the lost boys of this century. History will reflect that several generations of African American men stood by and allowed African American boys to become prisoners in their own public schools, majority occupants and owners of a repressed society, and cellar dwellers. On this one, I expect very few arguments. As a people, we are in denial. As an identifiable subgroup, African American boys are in trouble, and I do not mean Band-Aid trouble.

Dr. Theman Taylor, a distinguished professor of History at the University of Central Arkansas in Conway, has long been a personal friend and mentor. One of his more prolific sayings is that if you identify a problem, you must have the audacity to propose a solution and make a real effort to change the thought process.

I know, addressing a societal problem isn't always a popular conversation starter, but what are the alternatives? To not have any dialogue and watch the numbers come back at the bottom year after year after year? We start here, today.

As we reflect on low-achievement in the public schools, we continuously talk the test chatter. Subgroups, disparities, LEP. And yet in urban schools like the ones in greater Pulaski County, the problem is that while the top achievers move, the bottom stands still. Do you know who occupies the bottom? African American males. Lowest academic achievement: African American males. Highest disciplinary referral group: African American males. Lowest college entrance exam taker: African American males. Poorest ADA: African American males.

This point of light is for you. Academic achievement will always reflect a disparity until black males move from the bottom toward the top. Although it forces the system to address this subgroup, NCLB will be for naught as the majority of school-age urban black males will still fail and drop out of the public educational system in alarming numbers.

As African American people, we clearly understand an undereducated sub group will have few opportunities in competitive job markets that require and almost demand over-educated applicants. To change this trend, I propose the radical ideal of African- American men of all walks of life, assuming responsibility for the posterity of their communities. We absolutely must form a Cross Sectional African American Male-Mentor Project. That means multiple partners working for the same causes. In this case, one singular cause. We must address the rage that's destroying the communities we all live in. When the playing field is equal, African Americans men have to assume some responsibility for the successes and failures of our children, especially African American boys.

African American communities and their so-called leadership must take control of their problems. We can't keep calling them "our people," and only pay attention to "their" needs during the election cycle. When groups of black men pose for the camera, and identify themselves as twenty-five strong ministers, and one-hundred outstanding this, and fifty for the future, what are they really talking about? The end result appears to be…. not much. It's great PR, but it is a con, a fraud, against our children. They don't need your few civic dollars at Christmas. Our kids need daily help.

When black males have a greater chance of being incarcerated before the age of twenty-five than going to college, then society as a whole has a problem. It is a daunting picture. Imagine a great picture without the proper contrast. As we speak of contrast, it is not White America that Blacks should fear. That picture has been replaced by the young African American boy wearing his pants around his knees, a grill in his mouth, his hat turned sideways and most importantly, one who reads and does math at an eighth grade level when he's nineteen years old. That should frighten the hell out of all of us.

Our Solution

We must increase the capacity by turning up the *AAMMP,* "The African American Male Mentors Project. We must start earlier and reach African American boys before they get to high school because, by then, it is too late. Two years ago, I started an elementary program called Four4theFuture. Our goal is to mentor fourth graders for five consecutive years until they're freshmen in high school. To accomplish this, we recruited college-age African American males to adopt a boy from the highest risk class – fourth grade African American boys – and spend one hour per week with that student for the next five years. Our young men must provide at least one hour per week of relationship building. But unlike other programs, we expect mentoring to continue throughout the whole year.

We collaborate with the principals, counselors, and invite parents to identify the highest-need students and make referrals during the early weeks of school. No school activity is off limits: registration, open house, school carnivals. We recruit so-called Blue, White and Black collar brothers to donate one hour a week to contact and encourage "their" posterity. The rest is simply relationship building. Commit to having lunch one day a month during the school year and the summer with an at-risk young black male.

I am more than happy to share this very simple plan to increase the capacity for young black men, and I will let the self-appointed and anointed leadership borrow from my get-it-done book. Start by showing up and not "showing out" in elementary schools. Volunteer for PTAs, and help the schools encourage the kids. Get black boys on course for college starting in middle schools by encouraging them to take PRE-AP classes and tutoring them or requesting a tutor if necessary. Push the four-year plans in the eighth grade to include AP courses like Calculus, AP Literature, and at least two years of productive Spanish or Foreign languages. We must keep African American males away from fluff courses that do not prepare them *for the college of their choice.*

Then, when the playing field is level, lose the White-

America-at-fault mentality. It is counterproductive with an equal playing field. Prepare like your parents did for a world that has the potential to be unfair. Black parents and the so-called black community leaders must assume responsibility for the outcomes associated with African American males NOW.

No one is oblivious to the fact that other ethnic groups and genders need attention as well. But, in order to progress as a community, a state, and a nation, we must address the bottom with a real plan of action. Not the top, nor the middle, but the bottom, and that is exactly where a majority of African American males in public education are. Again, I do not expect much argument here. Most people hate controversy, and will readily admit that it is easier to ignore instead of dealing with any issue that has "explosive" written all over it. The saying "he is on his own" is leading him closer to your yard every single day.

For those who do just fine living in denial, keep preaching to your 1000 plus members churches, and keep driving your fancy imported cars. Keep those starched business shirts pressed and creased. Keep having those fancy lunches with business executives, and politicians, and don't look back. Then shame on you, you, and you too.

The message you and others just like you send is exactly why the young African American males will continue to maintain society's status quo. More in prison than in college, more single mothers, and more sisters that accepts mediocre, instead of demanding good fathers and husbands. If nothing else motivates you to finally assume the responsibility of helping mentor a young African American male in the public schools, keep this thought close to you. Your daughters deserve better. You can hear me now, or hear her later.

It's time to increase the capacity and turn up the *AAMMPerage* now; the sooner, the better.

Chapter Twenty-One

A Call to Action

Ultimately, black male educators must act as the impetus for change and the medium by which efficacy becomes a standard in public education.

Dr. Walter Milton Jr.

A Matter of Life and Death: Why Black Men Must Save Black Boys in America's Public Schools. What a powerful call to action. Today we have a nefarious crisis to say the least. It appears that this nation has turned its back on young black men at a time when new housing developments known as prisons are increasing at a rapid pace. Mass incarceration is growing rapidly right before our eyes while many have just rendered themselves helpless. This is especially true in many public schools across the United States. It has been often said that, "Many of our schools have become a pipeline for the lucrative prison system that is increasing daily." A plethora of school districts throughout the country have no idea how to combat the academic deficiencies that are impacting black male students. One can claim that not all black male students are doing poorly, and I agree with that assertion 100 percent; yet, it is very clear that the majority of black males are struggling academically.

Many educators realize that school communities are now faced with achievement issues in ways they never were before. In both public and private institutions, access to quality instruction is not a guarantee for **_all_** children. Nevertheless, the overwhelming civic expectation is that children and youth grow to be productive citizens through the methodology of "schooling": a context that should provide excellent opportunities for self-growth and intellectual development. In essence, "schooling" becomes a necessary pathway, next to "parenting" and "spirituality," for young black males to reach their maximum potential. However, the road to success can be unnecessarily arduous unless young black males participate in developmental experiences that include being mentored by motivated persons who will provide them with a well-structured and comprehensive system of academic and social support.

There has been a relentless effort to shed light on what I feel is an important discussion: the plight of black males in general and in particular, the vicissitudes that they experience in public education throughout the United States. These two issues are inexplicably tied together because oftentimes one's educational experiences, accomplishments and merit attainment drive his or her quality of life and sometimes, outcome.

There is a tremendous need for high-quality PK-12 educational services in America. The ever-growing "gaps" that exist within American public education has generated much of the necessity. Many effective black male educators can easily identify several points of disparity such as school leadership, academic achievement, teacher professional development, black male student potential, literacy and language acquisition, school board governance, fiscal management, early childhood education, and the overall systems of schooling. Nevertheless, and more particularly, a variety of research in academic and mainstream journals has been written on the achievement gaps of black male students and the need to close such gaps in reading and math. As a matter of fact, many of the tenets of *No Child Left Behind* were developed using research data that exposed the shameful teaching and learning realities that many black male students and children living in poverty faced on a daily basis.

Here are a few examples of current disturbing trends in our educational system:

- Only 2 percent of the nation's 14,600 Superintendents are Black-American (2006)
- 68 percent of black-American children enter kindergarten with no preschool experience

- Black preschoolers are twice as likely to be expelled as Hispanic and white preschoolers
- Black fourth graders nationally score on average 26 to 35 points behind white students in state mandated reading and math assessments
- Black eighth graders nationally score on average 35 to 40 points behind white students on state mandated reading and math assessments
- In 2000, 65 percent of black male high school dropouts in their 20s were jobless
- In 2004, 72 percent of black male high school dropouts in their 20s were jobless
- At least 50 percent of the unemployed are functionally illiterate
- 43 percent of adults at the lowest levels of literacy are living in poverty
- 75 percent of the nation's prison inmates do not have a high school diploma
- The likelihood of being on welfare is inversely proportional to literacy levels

Essentially, we recognize that a national paradigm shift must take place in American public education. It is our contention that "school" is not just a place where children acquire a set of prescribed facts and figures; but it is also a place where young people begin to discover their individuality and become aware of their connection to humanity. As an educator, I am dedicated to improving "human life" through the medium of excellent educational programming for students and professional practitioners.

Black male students deserve a cache of services that focus on students achieving in school both academically and socially. We must address the challenges that school administrators face in a culture centered on accountability through standardized assessments. We have to hone in on the need to improve pedagogical programming for all children, but particularly, black males. We must emphasize the need to improve the early educational experiences of black male students so that the potential for success in school is greater. Schools must offer training development for governance entities and those administrators who are responsible for the fiscal management of schools and districts. Ultimately, black male educators must act as the impetus for change and the medium by which efficacy becomes a standard in public education.

This is a crucial time in history; serendipity is truly at play. It is evident that the Creator has deemed the significance of shedding light on what appears to be a bleak situation impacting the lives of so many young brothers between the gates of America. However, I believe there is a strong sense of awakening that is taking place; I see this as an opportunity to expose some of the root causes that have created challenges and critical information that can help us heal and get back on the right track.

There is a resounding voice that is yelling at the top of the mountain "know thy-self." I have learned that there is a direct correlation with knowing oneself and breaking the psychological chains that can trap and bind one into submission to conditions that control one's thoughts and behaviors. Haki Madhubuti puts it very succinctly and clearly as follows:

People Black and stone.

Be careful of that which is designated beautiful

Most of us have been taught from the basements

of other people's minds.

Often we mistake strip-mining for farming

and that truly glows is swept under

the rug of group production.

It is accepted in America that beauty is

thin, long & the color of bubble gum.

Few articles generated by the millions are beautiful

except people.

Trust people

One by one

the darker they come

the more you can give your heart,

Their experiences most likely are yours

or will be yours.

Even within the hue and hue less

Among them are those
Who have recently lost their ability to re-call;
They can hurt you
drop you to your knees with words
much of that which blast from their mouths
is not them the offense is
they do not know that it is not them
as they rip your heart open
And reduce you to the enemy.

I am most certain that experiences impacting black males collectively are spiritual, historical and cultural. Martin Luther King, Jr., once said that: "We are tied together in a garment of mutual destiny." We are a collective people who have been conditioned to operate individually because we have been taught information from others who do not necessarily have our best interest at heart.

I remember years ago that my mother told my siblings and me to get well acquainted with Deuteronomy chapter 28. She said within this chapter lies a great deal of wisdom as it pertains to the blessings and the curses and the obedience to God. Now that I am a grown man, I can see as clear as day what my mother was trying to convey. She used to say that, "Everyone knows who we are, but we do not know who we are, if we had a clue, we would stand up and be the great people that we are destined to be. We have a divine responsibility to learn and value our culture."

In verse four of Deuteronomy chapter 28, it reveals the blessings when we are obedient to God, "Blessed shall be the fruit of thy body," however, in the same breath, verse 18 reveals if we are disobedient to God cursed shall be the fruit of our bodies. The fruit of our bodies are our children. Personally, I believe this is the reason why black men must intervene when it comes to rescuing black boys. Historically, our disobedience to God has placed us in the situation that we are currently experiencing today and this can be verified throughout this chapter. Black men are the only ones who can teach our young black males true obedience to God. We are the fathers, brothers, uncles, friends, cousins – and yes, we are our brother's keeper. Therefore, it becomes our responsibility to protect, educate, reform and rehabilitate our youth for they are our future. I would encourage all to familiarize themselves and study Deuteronomy chapter 28. Our history is rich, beautiful and filled with a lot of peaks and valleys. It comes in many forms and fashions. I have found a ton of information regarding people of African descent in the Old Testament; however, it required me to study and research things ferociously.

In the words of Brother Haki R. Madhubuti, "I will say to you that we are at war and that black men in America are being removed from the earth like loose sand in a wind storm. I will make you aware of our self-hating and hurting ways, I will glue your ears to those images you reflect which are not being loved." Brother Madhubuti's words are powerful.

He is relentless in his message. We have learned to harm ourselves in so many ways because we have forgotten who we are and where we came from; therefore, our journey to where we are going looks challenging, but I know we will get there.

Psalms 83, 1-5 reads: "Keep not though silence, O God: Hold not thy peace, and be not still O God for lo thine enemies make tumult and they that hate thee and have lifted up thy head, they have taken crafty counsel against thy people and consulted against thy hidden (unborn children), they have said come and let us cut them off from being a nation that the name of Israel may be no more in remembrance. They have consulted together with one consent. They are confederate against thee." Is this what is happening now? It really makes one think, the similarities are very loud.

I have served as a school superintendent for more than ten years. In every district where I have served, black male students have struggled at some level. Therefore, I have dedicated my life to ameliorate many of the barriers and challenges facing all students in general, and black males in particular.

I began my educational career as a teacher in two suburban school districts, after which I became an administrator in an urban district. My first superintendent opportunity was in a rural district and my last position was in an urban district with a "suburban flair." These experiences have proven invaluable on my journey in that it is very rare for an educator to have had experiences in districts with completely different dynamics.

I am a pioneer in that I was the first African American superintendent in two of the school districts, and also the youngest in all of the districts in which I served and am currently serving. It is worthy to mention also that I was the first African American male to teach in two New York suburban districts. Throughout these different experiences, there remains one constant: I have discovered that all children are beautiful, different and have potential for greatness in spite of their circumstances. I learned not to see where they are currently, but to see what they can become. I, too, as a young black child had the great fortune of someone seeing my possibilities.

I knew that in order for me to bring about change in the educational arena, I would become a superintendent. This interest was sparked from experiences I had in both high school and college. Another reason for wanting to become a school superintendent was, and still is, my love for children. Indeed, I am passionate about the art of teaching and learning. As a superintendent, I am able to assist in the development and implementation of policies and results.

Educating our children is serious business. It is indeed a matter of life and death. The awesome task of an educator is to teach not only to the cognitive-self but the social-self, the emotional self, the physical-self, the linguistic-self and the spiritual-self. Unfortunately, many black male students arrive at school every day with broken spirits. Proverbs: 18:14 states

"The spirit of a man will sustain his infirmity; but a wounded spirit, who can bear?"

Being a school superintendent is oftentimes a thankless job. It is not a glamorous position; it has many challenges, disappointments and moments of sheer loneliness. It is the only job on earth in which continued employment is contingent on not ruffling feathers. An aggressive approach to school reform can sometimes severely impact a superintendent's career. However, the superintendency also has its share of rewards, especially when one can create an environment where children are achieving. This type of leadership requires that one is willing to make tough decisions based on what is best for children even when it conflicts with the agendas of the adults to whom those children are entrusted.

I strongly believe that American society, in general, encourages and appreciates the value of a quality education. It has certainly been widely accepted that education is a vital tool necessary to create and sustain a thriving and forward-moving citizenry. In other words, our children's education must be secured and protected. I also strongly believe that all black male students are capable of learning. I am a product of this form of thinking. Again, I have dedicated my life to finding the means to make sure that all black male students with whom I come in contact take advantage of the opportunities to learn.

According to predictions, expectations and assumptions of others, my life's journey should not have become my today's reality. Unfortunately, there were scores of people who told me that I could not accomplish my goal of becoming a school superintendent by age thirty-five.

Historically, white men have served as superintendents and determined the educational outcomes of the nation's children. However, through what I call divine intervention, I became superintendent right on target according to my goals and aspirations.

If I had listened to all of the naysayers, although I do realize that they were speaking from the context of their experiences, I probably would have remained a principal, fighting feverishly to find a position in central administration somewhere in the United States. I identified some personal skill-building goals throughout my career to prepare myself for school superintendency. Being a visionary is critical; one must assemble and remain steadfast to his or her vision regardless of adversity or triumph. Again, be mindful not to absorb doubt or negative energy from others. You must have internal mechanisms in place that reject such forces and keep you positively focused at all times.

It is important to recognize and accept that the path to any position of executive leadership can be a very lonely place; therefore, establishing and maintaining relationships based on trust and honesty are paramount. Nurturing relationships can sustain you during times of turmoil.

Years ago, George Washington Carver introduced the Power of Positive Thinking and Discovery, a principle that can be the foundation for anyone's success. Our thoughts drive our actions and experiences. He said, "We get closer to God as we get more intimately and understandingly acquainted with the things He has created. I know nothing more inspiring than that of making discoveries for one's self." My mother always said, "The human mind is a powerful instrument." Understandably, it is imperative to program your mind to be goal-oriented and to concentrate on achieving those goals. It is my desire that black men will declare this and put this frame of thought within the grasp of black boys. Jawanza Kunjufu vehemently states: "We have to give our children, especially black boys, something to lose. Children make foolish choices when they have nothing to lose."

Ten Important Things to Say to Young Black Males

1. You are important and you matter:

When we look at the extremely alarming murder rates in our urban epicenters, it is of epidemic proportion. In cities like Detroit, Michigan for example, there were 375 homicides in 2012. The majority of the deceased were black males between the ages of 19 to 26. Similarly, there were over 500 murders in Chicago with the majority being Black males killing and being killed. Eighty-five murders in Atlanta and 113 homicides in St. Louis are just examples from a much more extensive and morbid list. This is even happening in smaller cities such as Flint, Michigan (66 homicides in 2012) and Rochester, New York (37 homicides). The street corners of many inner cities across the U.S. are serving as killing fields. Oftentimes our young men do not understand or feel that they are valued. We have to remind them that their lives are important. We have to remind them that historically they come from a culture of peace, non-violence and self-elevation, not destruction.

2. Preparation for your profession begins in the classroom:

Often, we are bombarded with problems that black male students face; we have heard and read about the endangered species model, pipeline-to-prisons phenomenon, chronic underachievement and the continuation of absentee fathers. All of these issues are the problems of our collective society, a burden that we all must bear. Academic excellence has to be the ultimate goal. We have to teach our young men about urgency and self-advocacy for them to do well and remain focused in school. They have to know that education is the key to potentially having a life of quality and success.

3. Learn how to read – and read well and read often:

Every student, regardless of his social or economic circumstance, deserves the right to be educated in a nurturing and well-structured learning environment. Students need to be encouraged to think freely, take chances and reach their full learning potential. If this is achieved then our society's future is brighter because of the well-prepared, self-aware and self-determined adults who hold the welfare of our society in their hands. Therefore, we have to ensure that our schools are more than just a place to go. Our schools must foster the successful growth of our students' mental capabilities, social attitudes, emotional health, physical fitness, language proficiency, integrity and character. To accomplish this, we have to make sure that all of our students have access to a quality education. We have to emphasize the importance of literacy to our young men. Literacy is key and reading has to be fundamentally first in our homes and our schools. Having high expectations for our young men is vital. If they feel safe, secure and loved, our young men have a unique way in which they work diligently to meet high expectations.

4. Words have power; and our word is our bond:

We have to teach our young men the importance of embracing integrity, honesty, commitment, responsibility and character. My father used to say to me, "Your actions are so loud that I cannot hear a word that you are saying." This was often a reminder that one was not following through with things that he/she would promise. "Your actions are much louder than words." People have a tendency to lose faith in you if you do not follow through with your plan of action. If you say that you are going to do something, do exactly what you say you are going do, or do not make a false promise! Your credibility can be lost and people will eventually lose trust in you.

5. What you give is what you will receive (Law of Reciprocity):

Our young men have to understand that their actions have consequences. I am a firm believer that when you do well by others, the probability of great things happening to you increases; immensely.

6. Establish goals and work your plan:

There is an old saying that many people are familiar with, "A journey of a thousand miles begins with the first step." Having goals and plans are essential components that lead to success. Often we mistake movement with progress; yet, there could be a great deal of movement, but no progression towards a desired outcome or goal. We have to teach our young men to be focused so they do not let the distractions of life interfere or deter them from their goals and objectives.

7. To be early is to be on time; to be on time is to be late:

We have to teach our young men the value of promptness. They have to understand that they can miss out on an opportunity or experience some type of disadvantage because of their lateness. Also, being on time helps promote respect for others, whether it is school, business, or life in general. People have a tendency to measure you based on your ability to be on time.

8. You may have made mistakes, but you are not a mistake:

So many of our young men come from homes where there were unplanned pregnancies, foster parents or single parentage that led to their being subjected to ridicule, negativity and poverty. This may lead one to believe that they are a burden or unwanted. These young men may be tempted to turn to the streets for status, notoriety, respect and a sense of belonging. Our young men may make mistakes, but they are not mistakes. They are children of God; therefore, they are blessings and they should be treated as such. We have to remind them of this daily.

9. Differentiate the pain of discipline versus the pain of regret:

It takes discipline to walk away from situations that appear to be attractive but not healthy and in many instances, inappropriate and sometimes illegal. The consequences of participating in unwarranted behaviors can lead to regret.

Hard work truly pays off; there is no substitutes or quick fixes. Discipline and consistency lead to success.

10. Man does not decide his future; habits decide his future:

We have to teach our young men that they are in charge of their destiny with the help of God and their choices. Our young men must take advantage of opportunities that will advance them in life. However, we must teach them to recognize the differences between opportunity and mistakes.

Afterword

Sam McNabb

As a father who has raised two African American males, I personally understand the urgency surrounding this most important topic about our boys and today's educational system. Although my biological sons have turned out to be very successful, I am still concerned about young men who need guidance, mentoring, direction and fathering. I have dedicated my life to offering assistance to young men so that they can overcome the many forces that they must contend with throughout their lives. As such, this book and the kernels of wisdom embedded in it are a Godsend.

I have worked extensively with a national initiative entitled "Boys to Men." The more I interface with young men, the more I realize that I have to be a broker of hope. Hope is the major theme that ties all of these essays together. Hope is paramount as we individually and collectively influence the lives of the young men who have been assigned to us.

Many people realize that our communities are bombarded with issues that erode at the fabric of our society. In both public and private institutions, access to quality education is not a guarantee for all children. As the authors so eloquently point out, "Nevertheless, the overwhelming civic expectation is that children and youth grow to be productive citizens through the methodology of 'schooling'; a context that should provide excellent opportunities for self-growth and intellectual development. In essence, 'schooling' becomes a necessary pathway, next to 'parenting' and 'spirituality', for American children to reach their maximum potential." I concur with this 100 percent.

As the authors contend, "We are aware that historically, American political and social conditions in public education have created a 'mosaic of gaps', especially, as we look at the challenges that many African American male students are facing. This mosaic includes achievement gaps, expectations gaps, opportunity gaps and income gaps, to name a few. Within the last ten years, the American achievement gap in reading and mathematics among Caucasian and African American children has been extensive."

Furthermore, I agree with Dr. Milton that: "Every student, regardless of their social or economic circumstance, deserves the right to be educated in a nurturing and well-structured learning environment, where they will be encouraged to think freely, take chances and reach their full learning potential. If this is achieved, then our society's future is brighter because of the well-prepared, self-aware and self-determined adults who will hold the welfare of our society in their hands."

I am so excited that Dr. Milton and Dr. Nellums felt compelled to shed light on what is happening to African American male students in America's Public Schools.

They, along with the various men who have contributed to this project, have provided parents, educators, students and community stakeholders with blueprints for success.

What these writers did was not only remarkable, but also replicable. Every young black boy who picks up this book can see him self mirrored in the stories, narratives and testimonies that illuminate from its pages. We, as a community and as a nation, can no longer excuse away the destructive behavior that has engulfed our communities.

It goes without saying that this book has impacted my life in a meaningful way. It has intensified my desire to advocate and it has compelled me to do even more. I encourage these authors to continue to delve deeper into the topic of black boys and education.

I commend them for having the passion, courage, focus and perseverance that was needed to guide the development and implementation of this project. I am confident that everyone who reads this book will be excited and dedicated to making a difference. Collectively, we can create homes, schools and communities where black boys excel and live up to their potential not only be successful, but to be great men!

For more information and to order additional copies, please visit: www.oneLgroup1.com or Amazon.com.